The publisher gratefully acknowledges the generous support of the Lisa See Endowment Fund in Southern California History and Culture of the University of California Press Foundation.

Luminos is the open access monograph publishing program from UC Press. Luminos provides a framework for preserving and reinvigorating monograph publishing for the future and increases the reach and visibility of important scholarly work. Titles published in the UC Press Luminos model are published with the same high standards for selection, peer review, production, and marketing as those in our traditional program. *www.luminosoa.org*

Water and Los Angeles

Water and Los Angeles

A Tale of Three Rivers, 1900–1941

William Deverell and Tom Sitton

UNIVERSITY OF CALIFORNIA PRESS

University of California Press, one of the most distinguished university presses in the United States, enriches lives around the world by advancing scholarship in the humanities, social sciences, and natural sciences. Its activities are supported by the UC Press Foundation and by philanthropic contributions from individuals and institutions. For more information, visit www.ucpress.edu.

University of California Press
Oakland, California

Cover illustration: Crowds at the 1913 celebration of Owens River water finding its way to Los Angeles. From the C. C. Pierce Collection of Photographs, photCL Pierce 06844, courtesy of The Huntington Library, San Marino, California.

Suggested citation: Deverell, William and Sitton, Tom. *Water and Los Angeles: A Tale of Three Rivers, 1900-1941*. Oakland: University of California Press, 2017. doi: http://doi.org/10.1525/luminos.21

Library of Congress Cataloging-in-Publication Data

Names: Deverell, William, author. | Sitton, Tom, author.
Title: Water and Los Angeles : a tale of three rivers, 1900–1941 / William Deverell and Tom Sitton.
Description: Oakland, California : University of California Press, [2016] | Includes bibliographical references and index.
Identifiers: LCCN 2016028675 (print) | LCCN 2016031387 (ebook) | ISBN 9780520292420 (pbk. : alk. paper) | ISBN 0520292421 (pbk. : alk. paper) | ISBN 9780520965973 ()
Subjects: LCSH: Water-supply—Los Angeles—History—20th century. | Rivers—California—Los Angeles—History—20th century. | Los Angeles (Calif)—History—20th century.
Classification: LCC HD4464.L7 D48 2016 (print) | LCC HD4464.L7 (ebook) | DDC 333.91/620979409041—dc23
LC record available at https://lccn.loc.gov/2016028675

26   25   24   23   22   21   20   19   18   17
10   9   8   7   6   5   4   3   2   1

CONTENTS

PREFACE

The two of us have been thinking and writing about Greater Los Angeles for a long time. Some of this work pertains to projects we have pursued separately: scholarly articles and books on this or that theme or topic pertaining to the history of Southern California. But much of what we've done has been collaborative as friends and colleagues. We edited a collection of essays about Progressive Era California; we brought out a volume devoted to the 1920s in Los Angeles and all its attendant growth and cultural busyness. We worked together on a biography (which Tom authored) on Los Angeles harbor and transit pioneer Phineas Banning.[1]

Through many joint projects such as these, as well as what amounts to an extended conversation stretching across many years, we have studied and thought about various facets of the institutional and infrastructural growth of the metropolis from the beginning of the American period forward. We approach the subject and themes of Los Angeles history differently, but those differences have been, in every instance, mutually reinforcing and, we think, enriching to our readers and students.

Like they all seem to be, this project has been several years in the making. We knew that the primary source material on Los Angeles growth and metropolitan ambitions was rich and evocative and needed wider circulation among students. We also knew that the environmental history of Greater Los Angeles stood as a remarkably complex, hugely important feature of the history of the region, of California, of the nation, and of the world.

Hence this project. In the pages that follow, we examine the growth of Los Angeles by way of the three rivers that play critical and fundamental roles in supplying freshwater to the landscape and its many millions of people. Our focus is on a riparian triptych: the Los Angeles River, the Owens River, and the Colorado River. They are, each in its own way and together as an interconnected system, of paramount importance to the history and the future of the region we call home. In this volume, we limit our investigation of each river to a discrete and relatively short time period, from the start of the twentieth century to the coming of the Second World War. The era from World War II to the present is unquestionably important to the riparian history of metropolitan Los Angeles. We cast our analytical net earlier, however, because we believe that this four-decade period is especially critical to how Greater Los Angeles brought each river, in both different and related ways, to bear on the global future of Southern California. Perhaps a subsequent volume will pick the story up from the 1940s and carry it forward to the recent past. To be sure, the rivers and the ways in which they roll through Los Angeles and through Los Angeles history deserve far more than a single scholarly examination.

We do not think that histories of these three rivers—so alike in some ways and so profoundly different at the same time—have ever been put together in the ways we try to do in this book. That seems odd to us: a missed, critical opportunity and obligation to deepen understanding about the region and the environmental and other challenges it faced in the past and which are growing more difficult with each passing year. Without the Colorado, the Owens, and the Los Angeles, there is no modern Los Angeles. Such a simple truism and statement of fact is but the first—important—insight about the region and its rivers. More complicated, and hardly less important, is to try to understand how and why the region developed such a complex technological, fiscal, political, and environmental relationship with three entirely different and diffuse riparian systems. The stories of Los Angeles and its namesake river, the stories of Los Angeles and the Owens River, and the stories of Los Angeles and the Colorado River are historical narratives that illuminate and illustrate broad sweeps of western and American history.

That's the purpose of this book—to know a region's rivers and the ways in which those rivers explain historical change of gargantuan proportion *and* to know about broad themes in American history that these water stories illustrate and highlight. The prisms we bring to the river history of Southern California—political, environmental, technological—help us figure out the regional past and, at the same time, help us place the region into wider frames of western, national, and even international history.

Putting this book together has been a pleasure, and we hope and expect that the documents (for the most part in their original grammar and syntax) and images that follow will help you think about, ask about, and better understand the Southern California past. We hope, too, that in so doing you will find ways to think creatively about the Southern California present and future.

William Deverell and Tom Sitton
San Marino, California

Introduction

It all happened very fast. In but two generations, Anglo-Americans and the wildly expansive American nation established dominion over the arid landscapes of the far West (and the indigenous inhabitants who lived upon them) through inter-related, mutually reinforcing processes of conquest and violence. The brief and brutal war with Mexico (1846–48), a giant land grab ineptly disguised as a pa-triotic defense of national sovereignty, brought the *entire* northern third of the Republic of Mexico into U.S. possession, with California as the great prize. At the very moment of territorial cession, the discovery of Sierra Nevada gold suggested to many an American that Manifest Destiny's fervent presumption—that God wished Americans and America to expand continentally from sea to sea—had been revealed and forever validated in the instant that it took startled James Mar-shall to pluck a small gold nugget from the millrace at Sutter's mill in Northern California. "I have found it," he said, and the world changed in the instant of his saying so.

Our focus here in this book is on what we might call the next phase or phases of that conquering era, the consolidation and further incorporation of territory in the latter half of the nineteenth century and the early years of the twentieth. In-stead of concentrating on gold and Northern California, we look here to Southern California, with a tight focus on water and the ways in which control of water is at the very foundation of Southern California's meteoric rise to metropolitan power about a century ago. Just as the nation grew at a remarkable pace by way of territo-rial ambition and warfare with Mexico and Native America, so, too, did Greater

Los Angeles explode—in ways more urban and suburban than bellicose—from the latter nineteenth century through the early twentieth. Water is at the heart of that process (and, to be sure, *battles* over water), and the growth of the nation, growth of the West, and growth of Los Angeles are intricately linked and concentric examples of many of the same phenomena.

This book is about that single city, its namesake county, the hinterlands stretching in three compass directions from both, and the freshwater on and under all those millions of acres of land. It is at once a story about Los Angeles and Greater Los Angeles and a story about the four decades leading up to the Second World War. One fact to keep in mind: Los Angeles becomes *greater Los Angeles* in so many ways precisely because of water. Metropolitan growth depended on all kinds of ingredients; water was certainly high on that list. With water came growth. That sounds simple, but it was not.

This is also a story about the far West, about its mountains, deserts, and flat landscapes. And at its heart, this book, like this story, is about how the control over three rivers *made* modern Los Angeles. Those three rivers are the *Colorado,* the *Owens,* and the *Los Angeles.* They are entirely and utterly different; the Los Angeles River is tiny, the Owens River is (or was) pretty big, and the Colorado River, the mighty Colorado, rolls through a watershed that draws in seven states and a lot of northern Mexico. But as a Goldilocks fable put together as history, these rivers—one small, one medium, and one gigantic—tell a linked story about *all* the issues of growth and politics important to the entirety of the modern American West.[1]

Our project is about the past, and we conclude our investigation as the Second World War commences. But do not be mistaken. The water story is a story saturated in the relationship between past and future. As the twenty-first century deepens, water is only going to get more important in the West. Growth, pollution, climate change: these are all now intertwined in complicated ways such that water—its availability, its reliability, its price, its conservation, and how it travels from point A to point B, not to mention point Z—is increasingly at the forefront of political decision-making and political tussles in Southern California (and everywhere else in the West and Southwest).

Our approach in this volume is to put water and history together. Understanding how water sources and systems have been envisioned, corralled, captured, toyed with, fought over, and championed is fundamental to fostering awareness and knowledge of contemporary or upcoming challenges. The history of water, as it relates to the history of Los Angeles, is not just interesting. It is vital. We have to understand key features of that history so that we can better understand what the constantly changing world of water means in contemporary Southern California and, by extension, across the vast expanses of the West.

MAKING SENSE OF WATER AND THE SOUTHERN
CALIFORNIA PAST

Given the chronological focus of this volume—forty years or so, from the beginning of the twentieth century to the coming of the Second World War, we want
students to gain a lot of insight into the periods of U.S. history generally bracketed
as the Progressive Era—1900–1920—and the New Deal era, from 1930 to the coming of the World War. We think that exploring water in the West, and especially
water in Southern California, is an ideal way to do that. Why? Because the issues
that help us define and understand these eras (and "the Twenties" in between
them) are brought into very sharp focus with investigation of the history of water
development in Southern California as it relates to each of the three rivers this
book tracks.

A review of some of those themes and big concepts is in order. From there, you
will be able to contemplate them more fully as you read sections of this book and,
especially, the documents that we have selected for each of those sections.

American historians mark the Progressive Era as, more or less, the period encompassing the first twenty years of the twentieth century. This kind of dating
can be arbitrary, and it has a lot to do with the ease and convenience of decadal
brackets (the 1920s, the 1930s, and the like). We can find ways in which the 1890s
exhibit facets and features of proto-Progressivism, just as we can find aspects of
Progressivism that cross the divide between 1920 and what comes after in the eras
of the Great Depression and New Deal. Nonetheless, this two-decade chunk at the
start of the new century is a reasonable bracketing of a complex period of reform
and change within American society and politics.

Progressivism constituted a broad range of ideas, faiths, beliefs, actions. And
the personnel invested and interested in Progressivism constituted a broad and
diverse lot. Some things stand out, however, and historians are in general agreement about them. For one, progressives (we make a distinction between progressives, as a general political category, and Progressives, or those who pledged
allegiance to the Progressive Party)—often optimistic, often idealistic, mostly
middle-class professionals, mostly white, mostly men, mostly urban (with important exceptions to each of those "mostly" assumptions)—wished to harness
the power of government so as to put an end to, or at least to arrest the political
will to perpetuate, the extremes of the previous era's runaway moneymaking and
enshrinement of industrial capitalism and industrial capitalists. What concerned
many a progressive was the gilt and excess of the Gilded Age, that era which
had drifted from the late nineteenth century into the twentieth: too much in the
hands of too few, unregulated industrial expansion, immigrant and other labor-
ers risking life and limb in dangerous factories and sweatshops, cities that were
too crowded, too dangerous, too diseased.

Progressives aimed to bring order to chaos, to dial back on all the excess, to establish controls. One important way they wished to do this was through a regulatory recipe drawn from governmental response in oversight and enforcement of laws, often new laws that they put on the books. In other words, progressives recognized that the power and purse of government—local, state, and especially federal government—could provide the legal and enforcement brake upon the specter of industrial power run amok. And so they ran for office, they ran campaigns for office, they wrote and wrote and wrote, and they tried to figure out ways beyond inept or corrupt or otherwise "politics as usual" as they perceived them.

Progressives evinced an inordinate faith in expertise and technical prowess. Some of this looks naive to us now. Many a progressive championed technical or scientific prowess out of the charming belief that such training or experience *necessarily* lifted an individual beyond the reach of crass political or financial or other aims and motivations. One important legacy of progressivism is the early twentieth century's initiation of large-scale projects dependent on newly professionalized cadres of engineers, planners, and scientists. This faith in technology and a "technocracy" was evident in the Progressive and New Deal periods, connecting the early twentieth century and the New Deal's big engineering footprint across the entire United States, from the Grand Coulee Dam in the Northwest to the Tennessee Valley Authority in the Southeast and everywhere in between.

That embrace of, and faith in, technical expertise—which Progressives thought could be applied to politics itself by way of such innovations as the city manager system of executive government—undergirded a fervent desire to establish control over nature. This in turn relates to a generalized progressive desire to sculpt order from chaos and to bring hygiene atop all manner of dirt: dirty water, dirty politics, dirty bodies, dirty minds, and dirty bloodstreams, with all that those fears entailed in reflexive and ugly racial and moral presumptions.

Control of nature, which we can see in all three of our river case studies about Progressive and New Deal Los Angeles, nestled right up against faith in the necessity of public ownership and management of natural resources.[2] Fearful that the messy and inefficient excesses of capitalism and capital markets would sully and impinge the efficient delivery of such commodities as water and electricity, progressives worked hard to bring natural resource exploitation into regulatory order and public oversight.

How and where do we see these themes playing out in the far West? That's easy: all over the place, in all kinds of instances and initiatives—whether in campaigns to reform the approach to incarceration and education in the juvenile delinquency system in Denver, or in early and important campaigns for women's suffrage in the Rockies. (Progressives were generally in favor of suffrage for women, however caricatured the reasons, in that they believed that the impact of women's votes would be uplifting, even soothing, in the hurly-burly of politics.) In our case-study region of Southern California, the engineering feats attached to the histories of the three rivers under scrutiny are nothing short of extraordinary. Holding the Los Angeles River in place by a concrete hug was a new thing in the early decades of the twentieth century. Bringing a big river 250 miles to Los Angeles, by gravity, was an incredible feat in the same era. And tugging the Colorado River west and north of the route it wanted to take to the Pacific Ocean, by way of an aqueduct system so that it watered Greater Los Angeles' mouths and fields, lawns and swimming pools, brings in visions of the Roman Empire in terms of design, execution, and impact. Add to that last effort the imagining and eventual building of Hoover Dam, and the story becomes a set of grand riparian actions at the instigation and scale of a civilization.

Building great things, or at least building great big things, does not make a society great. Certainly, it does not come with moral congratulations as accompaniment to a high regard for, even awe at, the achievements themselves. Hoover Dam is a great engineering feat. But is Hoover Dam great? Is the control of the Colorado River great? Is the Los Angeles Aqueduct great? Is Los Angeles great? We have a lot of analytical, historical, and other work to do before we can grapple successfully with such questions as these.

Where does all this leave us? How, at river's edge, or at rivers' edges, can we learn about the way things work in the far West? How, with attention upon river histories, can we better understand the way to move forward into a world changed by climate differences, irrevocably changed and challenged by the fact of too little water for too many demands?

DOWN BY THE RIVERS

As a way to organize our investigation, think of three circles, one inside the other, each touching upon or wrapping around parts or all of Southern California. At the center is the local setting and local stories that are tied to a single riparian landscape feature: the Los Angeles River. All history is, at some level, local history, and the Los Angeles River allows us to zoom into a highly localized landscape across reasonable dimensions of time and space. It is a little river flowing atop (and sometimes below) a big geologic basin, and it empties into the Pacific Ocean, if it ever gets that far, season to season, year to year.

The next circle of inquiry and geography spreading outward is a more state-focused view. That takes us out to the Owens River in southeastern California. That landscape has its own local stories and local lore, to be sure, but our focus here is on the ways in which the history of the Owens River, from about 1900 forward, helps us understand broad themes across a century of California history. It is a bigger river: it flows nearly two hundred miles through a valley created by the Sierra Nevadas on the eastern side and the White and Inyo Mountains on the west. By

FIGURE 1. Bucolic, tiny, seemingly innocuous: the Los Angeles River (and cattle) in the nineteenth century.
Photo photCL 49 (7f), courtesy of The Huntington Library, San Marino, California.

way of what is now a set of highly engineered delivery systems, the Owens River answers more than gravity's demands, running nowadays to the very edges of the city of Los Angeles.

Farthest out in our concentric reckoning is the Colorado River, and our investigation of its relationship to urban and suburban growth brings us to the national and international level of analysis. The Colorado is a giant river, flowing nearly fifteen hundred miles through the center of an immense watershed, where it has carved out astonishing canyons and gorges across millennia, and where its history and flow influence millions upon millions of people.

We are accustomed to people taking each of these rivers on separate historical terms. We know of dozens of studies and tales that speak to time spent thinking about or rafting on the mighty Colorado River. The Owens River has its own adherents or mourners, as the case may be; and the tiny Los Angeles River elicits commentary, too, ranging from jokes to elegies. But we want to do something very different and not spend time or analytical energy on the rivers apart.

At least insofar as reference to Southern California is concerned, it is historically interesting and viable *not* to uncouple these three stories, these three rivers, from one another. They are linked—and it is also important to grapple with all three and their intricate and particular relationships to growth in the Greater Los Angeles region of the late nineteenth and early twentieth centuries.

Understand them, understand them *together*, and we will understand *a lot* about modern Los Angeles.

Let's begin locally, with the littlest river. Los Angeles grew up precisely because of the Los Angeles River. The river once began as a tiny stream that came up from underground springs in the San Fernando Valley and then, gathering surface water, meandered southerly toward the Pacific Ocean. The river often ran dry, or nearly so, in the hot summer months. Spanish explorers and settlers laid out Los Angeles near it and, as a result, very close to the indigenous habitations that had also risen up alongside the river. By the end of the eighteenth century, the river had been given a Spanish name, El Río de Nuestra Señora la Reina de Los Ángeles de Porciúncula, and from it was carved the name of the pueblo nearby. The tiny European outpost of Spanish colonialism and Catholicism grew slowly through the first decades of the nineteenth century, drawing agricultural and other water from the modest Los Angeles River by way of ditches *(zanjas)* or other means, such as water carriers. Anglo-American arrivals in the years before and after American conquest (1848) continued these practices, and the agricultural hinterlands just beyond the village boundaries grew with water the river supplied.

Up until about 1900, the Los Angeles River—surprisingly, given its temperamental, streamlike stature—supplied enough water, by way of its aboveground flow and the artesian wells that tapped into it, to fulfill most of the freshwater needs of Los Angeles and its immediate hinterlands. People drank the river, they watered their crops with it, used it as a sewer, tossed their household trash and other refuse, their dead dogs and dead horses (and occasional human dead), into the river in hopes that it would wash away or at least move conveniently downstream. Such has been the use of rivers since time immemorial, so it's no surprise that the Los Angeles River fared the same.

This river had long been fickle—disappearing when the weather was hot and dry, but at times, especially in winter months, giving in to floods. When heavy rains fell in the nearby foothills and San Gabriel Mountains, the precipitation could overwhelm the river's tributaries and the river itself, which had a tendency to spill over its banks and flood large sections of the Los Angeles basin, which had been scooped out like a bowl below the steep San Gabriel Mountains to the northeast.

At first, or at least for several late-nineteenth-century decades, this did not seem like such a big problem. The river flooded, it brought nutrient-rich silt into groves and agricultural fields, and it usually returned to its bed, where it occasionally just ran dry in the summer. At times, the river leapt from its bed and headed off in an entirely different direction. When it flooded, some land could be damaged, livestock or houses occasionally swept away, and human lives lost. But on the whole, those living in the basin had learned through time and experience to build away from the river's banks in anticipation of a flood every ten or so years.

FIGURE 2. Flooding, gently, into neighboring fields: the Los Angeles River through the Elysian Gap, late nineteenth century.
From the C. C. Pierce Collection of Photographs, photCL Pierce 06837, courtesy of The Huntington Library, San Marino, California.

That changed. Los Angeles grew so rapidly in the latter decades of the nineteenth century that Los Angeles River floods became much more problematic. Real estate excitement and speculation attached dollars and optimism to land; when some or a lot of that land washed away in the wintertime, that created a problem. And when, in the early twentieth century, two years (1914 and 1916) saw flooding of gargantuan proportions—floods that knocked out communication and transportation connections to the outside world—Angelenos decided that they had had enough.

That response, which we can characterize as an ambitious and largely successful attempt to exert muscular and modern technological control over nature, begins our local story about Los Angeles' growth and its riparian cultures.

At virtually the same time—and, again, it is important to think beyond coincidence—municipal leaders and institutions in Los Angeles began to look for a river better suited to the breathless ambitions of a city on the make. Early twentieth-century Los Angeles leaders—businesspeople, government officials,

FIGURE 3. Harsh floods—the 1880s.
Photo photST Tyler (1), courtesy of The Huntington Library, San Marino, California.

boosters of all stripes—often painted their city with hyperbole. Los Angeles would be, they shouted, the greatest American city of the twentieth century. Los Angeles would rival the great capital cities of the world. Los Angeles would triumph as the American contribution to urban life, culture, and success. On the one hand, it's easy to cut through much of this language and see it as overheated rhetoric laid atop crass commercial ambitions to sell Los Angeles, its land, its houses, its agricultural products, and its future to eager newcomers, visitors and settlers alike. But we ought to remember, too, that this kind of energetic selling of the future of Los Angeles had its counterpart in the actual reshaping of the landscape in ways every bit as ambitious, whether the exact consequences were intended or not. And it was the same in most U.S. cites at one time or another.

With the coming of the twentieth century, then, Los Angeles faced an ironic situation with its namesake river. On the one hand, the Los Angeles River, which could run dry in the summertime, did not look as if it were up to the task of supplying enough water for the people, the animals, the crops, and other needs of the growing metropolis. Having too little freshwater posed a big challenge to the growth machine that had already begun to flex its industrial, agricultural, tourism, and other muscles. On the other hand, come the wintertime rains, the little Los Angeles River could and did occasionally morph into an angry maker of dangerous and destructive floods. Big floods came in the 1860s, and again in the 1880s, as the Los Angeles River washed out its banks and pooled water across the basin for

FIGURE 4. The Los Angeles River floods in winter, 1914.
Photo photPF 09441, courtesy of The Huntington Library, San Marino, California.

weeks at a time. Houses washed away. Fields became caked with silt and debris. Livestock drowned. Roads and bridges disappeared.

When floods returned in the early years of the new century—rainfall in February of 1914 and 1916 again brought the river, as noted earlier, out of its channel—regional engineers and political leaders initiated ambitious plans to corral the usually little river, to hold it on the landscape, floods or no floods, eventually by way of a concrete straitjacket.

What a story! Ambitious metropolis sells land and the idea of land (and land bathed in year-round sunshine) to the world. The world begins to come in bigger and bigger numbers, a journey made easier by post–Civil War railroad expansion across the West. But danger lurks on that landscape, in the form of a seemingly innocuous water source. Rains come. The river leaps its banks. It destroys the very land that boosters and champions are selling, and it can be deadly as well. Nineteenth-century people are not generally swimmers. They drown.

What to do? Modest, or at least relatively modest, plans are hatched in early twentieth-century Los Angeles to prevent the worst from seasonal floods. Maybe, engineers suggest, the answer lies high in the canyons and arroyos of the nearby San Gabriel Mountains. These steep, geologically new mountains look down on the basin from just north of towns such as Pasadena and Arcadia, which were then starting to expand. If rainfall could be gathered there, some opined, at the point

FIGURE 5. Cement for paving the Los Angeles River, 1939.
Call No: "Dick" Whittington Collection, photCL Whitt 0909, courtesy of The Huntington Library, San Marino, California.

where gravity is prepared to rush it downstream to the tributary Arroyo Seco, and thence on to the Los Angeles River, the worst of the flooding could be avoided. The plan was to put small dams, or weirs, a couple of feet in length, at multiple (dozens, hundreds, more) sites in the nooks and crannies of the San Gabriel Mountains, at places where water could pool and percolate back into the earth before roaring a dozen or fifteen miles downhill to Los Angeles and creating havoc.

Not bold enough. And maybe it wouldn't work. Leaders in Los Angeles of a century ago could be faulted for many things—corruption, greed, intellectual and cultural provincialism among them—but the embrace of small plans and small planning options was not usually on that list. A series of check dams, as an idea and practice, was largely abandoned (though hikers can still see remnant dams in the mountains) in favor of something far, far more ambitious.

Why not glue the Los Angeles River in place? Why not concretize the petulant stream? And so it went. Bonds went up for sale, Angelenos bought them, and engineers went to work. It took the better part of a century, as we shall see, but in the end, the Los Angeles was forcibly adhered, by concrete adhesive, to the landscape it once roamed.

Look to our next circle radiating outward: the Owens River. A couple of hundred miles to the north and east of Los Angeles lies the Owens Valley, now well known as the landscape through which skiers and other year-round recreation enthusiasts pass on their way from Southern California to the Sierra Nevadas and places like Mammoth Mountain ski area. In 1845, an exploring party of Americans, which included one Richard Owens, wandered into the valley, and Owens left his name behind when he departed.

A river that, in its natural course, flows some two hundred miles, the Owens rises from snowmelt. It runs into—and drains—two valleys, the Long Valley and the Owens Valley, not far from Yosemite National Park and California's highest peak, Mount Whitney. The Owens Valley, bigger by far than Long Valley, is a long stretch of land lying in between the Sierra Nevadas and the White Mountains, about 250 miles to the northeast of Los Angeles. As the Los Angeles River threw regular fits of flood and tempestuousness, steady (and big) rivers such as the Owens beckoned thirsty, ambitious Angelenos. Especially smitten was William Mulholland, chief engineer of the city's water department. Bold, smart, self-made, and gruff, Mulholland knew more about the city's watercourses and water needs than anyone. By the early years of the twentieth century, Mulholland had begun a quiet investigation, along with his surveyors and hydrologists, into the idea of bringing a river so reliable, so clear, and so seemingly accessible as the Owens was to Los Angeles.

Such were the ambitions of the Progressive Era. See it, want it, take it. Or, as William Mulholland of Los Angeles put it even more succinctly in response to the completion of the Owens River Aqueduct in late 1913: "There it is. Take it." And that is precisely what happened. Voters in Los Angeles purchased bonds; bureaucrats in Los Angeles purchased water rights in the Owens Valley. Engineers—Mulholland chief among them—designed a brilliant metal straw that they stuck in the river and used for drawing water (water that the city of Los Angeles now owned) all the way to Los Angeles. That made the aqueduct (which they called the Los Angeles Aqueduct when it reached the city); and for a moment at least, proud and slaked Angelenos even allowed themselves to imagine that they had, in one fell riparian swoop, solved their water needs *for all time*. Such naïveté did not last; it fell away when "plenty" of water turned out to be "not nearly enough."

That the Owens River project and ambition required stealth, science, politics, and money is a given; look beneath many a water deal in the West and you'll find such things. But it is the Owens River story that spawned a classic of American cinema. Voilà! Decades later, screenwriter Robert Towne, attuned to history and noir fiction, and partnered with film director Roman Polanski, gave us *Chinatown* (1974).

In the pages that follow, we examine some of the real-life issues and stories that lurk behind the scenes and sayings of the film. The intricate *Chinatown* plot revolves around a conspiracy in which wealthy Los Angeles businessman Noah Cross plots to bring Sierra Nevada water to his recently acquired agricultural

FIGURE 6. William Mulholland surveys the water future of Los Angeles.
Courtesy of the University of Southern California, on behalf of the USC Libraries.

acreage in the northwest San Fernando Valley by murdering a man who opposes a $10-million bond issue to finance the building of an aqueduct and reservoir. Cross uses hired muscle and city personnel to enforce the secrecy and fraudulence of his plot. Private investigator Jake Gittes eventually uncovers the plot to convince Los Angeles taxpayers that drought necessitates that they pay for the transfer of water that would irrigate Cross's land, raise prices, and make him another fortune.

The conspiracy theory concerning the origins of the actual Owens Valley project evolved in the early 1900s as newspaper editor Sam Clover, local socialists, and others sensed a plot by regional capitalists to use public funding to enrich themselves. In 1910, the delightfully named William T. Spilman wrote a little booklet called *The Conspiracy,* which spelled out the ramifications of the theory, and which has been embellished by others (screenwriter Robert Towne most famously) ever since. Steven P. Erie, Abraham Hoffman, and other scholars have demonstrated that the

FIGURE 7. A portion of the Los Angeles Aqueduct spilling Owens River water into newly
claimed land attached to the city of Los Angeles.
From the William Deverell Collection, courtesy of William Deverell.

overall theory does not hold up. In brief, the syndicate—including newspaper pub-
lishers Harrison Gray Otis and Edwin T. Earl, railroad magnates Henry E. Huntington and E. H. Harriman, banker Joseph F. Sartori, developer L. C. Brand, and several
others—publicized their plans to develop agricultural land in the San Fernando Valley long before the aqueduct project was even a possibility. In fact, one invited investor, Dr. John R. Haynes, confided to Upton Sinclair that he had declined to join the
syndicate precisely because the water project was not mentioned, or even known of,
as he believed. The syndicate did not become aware of the aqueduct project until
city engineers had already decided to pursue it; one of the water department commissioners most likely passed along the inside information to them. After that, the
syndicate members acted as typical Angeleno boosters in campaigning for a project
that would advance the interests of the city as well as their own.

That said, there certainly was plenty of conflict of interest to go around, including on the part of a former Los Angeles mayor (Fred Eaton) who purchased land
in Owens Valley; a water commissioner who was also an investor in the San Fernando Valley (Moses Sherman); and an engineer working for the federal government and city of Los Angeles at the same time (J. B. Lippincott).

Our last circle outward: the Colorado River. Rising out of the Rockies, a river
famed in the history of the American West, the river that carved the Grand Canyon (first among so many spectacular gorges worn away by the river), and the river
explored so magnificently by one-armed explorer, scientist, and Civil War soldier
John Wesley Powell, the Colorado is a one-of-a-kind river of North America. At

FIGURE 8. Inside the Colorado River Aqueduct, under construction, early 1930s.
Courtesy of the Banning Library District, Banning, California.

nearly fifteen hundred miles long, it is about ten times the length of the Owens River and well more than twenty times bigger than the Los Angeles River. While the Los Angeles River drains but part of the Los Angeles Basin, and the Owens River drains the valley it rolls through, the Colorado River drains a great deal of the American West on the western slope of the Continental Divide.

Its sheer bigness has been, as we expect to show you, matched by the sheer and grandiose size of Southern California's designs upon it. For as the Los Angeles River gave way to the Owens River as the Los Angeles water source round about 1915, so, too, did the Owens give way to the Colorado two decades later. It was one thing for an ambitious metropolis to go after, and get, a snowpack river out of the mountains of the same state. It was another thing altogether for the region to set its sights on one of the world's great rivers. But set their sights Los Angelenos did, by means of legal innovation, treaty-making acumen, engineering prowess, and lots of money. By the beginning of the Great Depression, the Colorado River had been coaxed, legally and otherwise, toward Southern California, where it arrived by 1941. A consortial arrangement had been hammered out by which its waters would be further distributed, its energies converted to electricity, and its impact felt in the growing towns and neighborhoods of Southern California.

One, two, three: the Los Angeles, the Owens, and the Colorado. *A Tale of Three Rivers:* Los Angeles and Southern California as we know them come into being, get the water they need (though *never* enough), and in the process, launch stories, tales, animosities, careers, and pathos enough for a hundred novels and films.

1

Rivers of Growth

Gentlemen, today you can walk out that door, turn right, hop on a streetcar and in twenty-five minutes end up smack in the Pacific Ocean. Now, you can swim in it, you can fish in it, you can sail in it, but you can't drink it, you can't water your lawns with it, you can't irrigate an orange grove with it. Remember, we live next door to the ocean but we also live on the edge of the desert. Los Angeles is a desert community. Beneath this building, beneath every street, there's a desert. Without water the dust will rise up and cover us as though we'd never existed!

—LOS ANGELES MAYOR SAM BAGBY, *CHINATOWN*

If Los Angeles does not secure the Owens Valley Water supply, she will never need it.

—WILLIAM MULHOLLAND, *1906*

There it is. Take it.

—WILLIAM MULHOLLAND, *AT THE OPENING CEREMONIES OF THE LOS ANGELES AQUEDUCT, 1913*

Without water there would be no major growth for Los Angeles. Its Mediterranean climate can be very dry, and there are few sources of freshwater nearby. Sometimes there is too much water in the area: floods have destroyed homes and infrastructure, necessitating projects to control the floodwaters. At other times a lack of rain has caused the earth to dry up, destroying agricultural crops and limiting the amount of water available for thirsty city dwellers and suburbanites, not to mention future residents and industries. City officials and city boosters who promoted urban growth knew that they needed a dependable water supply and to control periodic winter flooding if Los Angeles was to grow to the size they envisioned.

In the early twentieth century, Los Angeles boosters and water seekers made the control of watercourses and the addition of new supplies a crusade for urban expansion. For the Los Angeles River, that meant maintaining and harnessing it to avoid costly damage. The Owens River would be acquired to expand the supply for a growing population in the near future; it became a major project, similar to the simultaneous construction of the Hetch Hetchy Dam, which would quench the thirst of San Francisco. Colorado River water would allow further expansion through a major federal project much like others that developed in, and developed, the West at this time. For Los Angeles, three rivers determined the pathways of growth in the early twentieth century, as the city swelled from a population of just over one hundred thousand in 1900 to the fifth largest in the nation by 1940.

. . .

THE LOS ANGELES RIVER

In the early stages of the Progressive Era many residents of Los Angeles became dissatisfied with the service of the private water company that held most of the city's freshwater supply. They were persuaded to vote for city ownership of water resources by engineers and boosters who feared the supply would not meet future demand as the city grew. Municipal ownership of some public resources became a progressive initiative throughout the nation and in Los Angeles, where the city would eventually add other resources to its list of assets and regulation in order to ensure orderly growth.

From "Municipal Ownership: Citizens' Committee on Water Bond Election Meet" (*Los Angeles Times,* August 18, 1899).

"MUNICIPAL OWNERSHIP

CITIZENS' COMMITTEE ON WATER BOND ELECTION MEET

PLAN OF CAMPAIGN TO GET OUT THE VOTE ADOPTED—QUESTION REVIEWED AND OPINIONS GIVEN. MEETING TO BE HELD THIS EVENING."

The Citizens' Committee of One Hundred met last evening in the Council chamber at the City Hall. The meeting was called to devise ways and means for getting a full expression of public opinion, regarding the municipal ownership of the waterworks, at the election for the issuance of bonds, to be held on Wednesday next. The meeting was an enthusiastic one, and another will be held this evening at 7:30 o'clock, at the same place.

Ex-Mayor Henry T. Hazard presided, and briefly stated the reasons for which the meeting was called. Maj. H. T. Lee, associate counsel for the city in the present water litigation, was called upon and reviewed the history of the Los Angeles water system. He said, in part:

"In the twenty-three years that I have lived in Los Angeles, I have been impressed with the persistence and vehemence of the contention of the citizens of the old pueblo that they owned the water supplied to the city. The city has owned the water ever since the town was nothing but a Mexican village. The proposition that the citizens of Angeles have to face is entirely different from the general question of the municipal

FIGURE 9. One section of the Los Angeles River in 1912 demonstrates its limitation as the primary source of water for a growing city.
Courtesy of the Los Angeles Public Library Photo Collection.

ownership of private utilities. Here we already own the water, the only point is, who shall control the supply?

"The coming election is to decide whether the city will vote the bonds necessary to discharge the contract which it entered into with the water company thirty years ago. No vituperation of the water company will avail, it is a plain business proposition. We must meet the water company face to face: fight every point, and establish our legal rights. To vote for the bonds is a duty, and no citizen should be negligent in discharging it." The speaker concluded by advocating that a fund be raised to give voters information regarding the location of voting booths.

Ex-Judge A. M. Stephens was the next speaker. In the course of his remarks he said: "It never occurred to me until confronted with the issue that it would be necessary to urge the people of Los Angeles to assume control of the water system. This system has meant a mint of money to the water company. All that we now have to do is buy the pipes. We already own the water."

·   ·   ·

Not all residents agreed that municipal ownership was called for or right. Some opposed a long-term bonding effort to purchase the Los Angeles Water Company; others opposed the takeover as anathema to the principle of private enterprise. The city's boosters, mostly political conservatives, were overwhelmingly behind the acquisition and campaigned diligently for its victory. The following are only two of many newspaper stories promoting the purchase.

From "The Opposition to the Bonds" (*Los Angeles Times*, August 27, 1901).

"THE OPPOSITION TO THE BONDS"

The opposition to the voting of the water bonds appears to be dwindling away, and it looks as if the bonds are likely to be carried by an overwhelming vote, unless, indeed, those who favor them should exhibit too much careless confidence, and stay away from the polls. Many a battle has been lost by overconfidence, or by underestimating the strength of the opposition.

There is no doubt whatever—as may be clearly seen from the numerous interviews that have been published in The Times—that a great majority of the voters of Los Angeles are in favor of paying the water company the $2,000,000 which it has agreed to accept, so as to bring to an end the apparently interminable litigation over the question, which a leading attorney recently declared could be prolonged by the water company, if it sees fit, for at least fifteen years. This is quite easy to believe, in view of the instances which come to light so frequently of legal controversies that have been drawn out to outrageous lengths, wherever one or both of the contestants happens to be possessed of the means to hire legal ability that has made a study of the multitudinous methods by which mills of justice may be prevented from turning out the grist too rapidly to suit their clients.

The lucid, complete and convincing reply prepared by the City Council to the obstructionist and published a few days ago in The Times, was undoubtedly the finishing stroke which settled the question definitely in the minds of a great many wavering voters, who have all along been in favor of the acquisition of the waterworks by the city, but were somewhat in doubt as to the possibility of doing so with safety and advantage to the community. A large number of these citizens—probably a great majority of them—fully agree with the opposition in their contention that the price to be paid for the water system is more than it is intrinsically worth, but, like sensible people, they recognize the fact that, through the loose and indefinite action of those who granted this franchise to a private corporation at a time when neither the city nor the corporation had the least idea of how valuable it was to become, we are, to a certain extent, at the mercy of the water company, and therefore the path of good judgment and good sense lies in the direction of the best compromise that can be made. This, again, is in the payment of $2,000,000 to the water company for all its rights, privileges and possessions.

From "Today will Decide Water Campaign" (*Los Angeles Times,* August 28, 1901).

"TODAY WILL DECIDE WATER CAMPAIGN:
FRIENDS OF BONDS, CONFIDENT OF SUCCESS IF VOTERS DO THEIR DUTY;
'LAST CARD' OF OPPOSITION"

Whether the city shall own and operate its waterworks now or hang on to the uncertainties of litigation, is the question to be decided at the polls today.

If the bonds carry, all pending litigation involving the waterworks will be terminated and the city will come into possession of the plant and its revenues as soon as the bonds are sold.

If the bonds fail, all compromise proceedings will be declared off and the city will again resort to legal measures to force the water company to a settlement.

Friends of the bonds will do well to remember that it takes a two-thirds vote to carry them and that one vote cast by the opposition will offset two ballots in favor of the $2,000,000 issue.

Voters will have an opportunity of recording their verdict from 6 o'clock A.M. to 5 o'clock P.M., during which hours the polls will remain open. The ninety general election precincts of the city have been grouped into twenty-nine municipal election precincts. A full list of the polling places and election officers was published in yesterday's Times.

FACTS TO BE CONSIDERED

A material reduction of water rates will be made possible by the purchase of the plant for $2,000,000. For the first few months, at least, the revenue from the plant will be diverted to making needed extensions to the waterworks. This work will employ only citizens and voters[,] and the State law provides that the minimum wage shall be $2 for eight hours' work.

If the $2,000,000 bond issue is voted, the Los Angeles City Water Company will allow judgment to be entered in all suits now pending in favor of the city and will sign such documents as will effectually secure the city in the ownership of the plant. This will put an end to the protracted and very expensive litigation which the city has carried on with this company for the last two years with slight success. Whereas, if the bonds fail, it is probable that the question will not be settled for the next fifteen years and the city will not only be out the revenue from the plant during that time, but will have heavy bills to pay for attorneys' fees and court costs.

When the city owns its waterworks, great prestige will be given it in suits involving riparian rights on the river. In all cases where the right of the city to claim the waters of the river has been involved, the specious argument has been made that, while the city had no waterworks it had no use *for* the water, and therefore could not plead necessity for the vital fluid on that score.

It should be remembered that the property covered by the compromise agreement is far greater than that included in the arbitrators' award of 1893. Then the main plant of the Los Angeles City Water Company was the only property under discussion. The compromise agreement of $2,000,000 covers the main plant, additional property of that company valued at $40,000 omitted from the arbitration, extensions since made costing $30,000 and the holdings of the Crystal Springs Land and Water Company and the East Side Springs Company. All the property included in the agreement has been valued by ex-City engineer Dockweiler at $1,988,000 or $12,000 less than the $2,000,000 which the city is asked to pay for the plant.

THAT INTEREST DODGE

The committee of the "antis," led by Waldron and Sherman Page, is seeking to make much anti-bond capital out of the provision in the agreement that allows the company 7 per cent interest on the $2,000,000 until final settlement is made. The same section of the agreement provides that the city shall come into the revenues of the plant at the time the bonds are officially canvassed, and it is determined that they have carried.

The gross revenue of the plant is over $38,000 per month, and the net revenue, or profit, is estimated at more than $25,000 per month. If the water company gets 7 per cent on the bond price, it will amount to $11,666 per month. Deducting this sum from the net revenues of the water plant leaves a balance of profit in favor of the city of $13,334 per month.

In case the compromise for any reason is not consummated, neither interest nor taxes will be paid on the plant by the city. In case the final payment of the $2,000,000 is delayed the city will be making a revenue of $18,334 per month until such time as control of the water plant is secured. Now the city is getting nothing. What more favorable agreement for the city could be secured?

LEADS TO LITIGATION

The only alternative offered by the anti-bondites is a return to the uncertainties of litigation. They may vote bonds in the sum of $884,000 and offer the money to the company. This will be refused and then the city can go ahead and build headworks.

But does not the average voter think that this would lead to a long and expensive court of litigation as the legality of such a tender would have to be determined? It may not be generally known, but there is now a suit filed in court testing the right of the city to do just this very thing. As the litigation has progressed up to this time[,] several years at least would be required to get a final decision in this case.

NOT MUNICIPAL OWNERSHIP

It is not a question of municipal ownership that is submitted to the voters at the polls today. That question was effectually decided when the city entered into the thirty-year contract in 1868. The city then bound itself to take over the plant at the expiration of the time, and entered into a contract that is equally binding on the city and the water company.

The trouble has arisen over the interpretation of that contract and its peculiar ver-biage, and the water company has effectually shown its ability to hang on to the plant and its revenues despite the efforts of the city. The reason why the water company is now willing to agree to a compromise is because the heavy expense of retaining three or four of the leading lawyers of the State has eaten into the profits to such an extent that the stockholders, or a majority of them, are willing to compromise for a reasonable sum.

On both the city and the water company the drain has been exceptionally heavy, and many well-informed persons state that they believe it for the best interests of both the water company and the city to compromise the existing difficulties.

WHAT MERCHANTS THINK

Further returns have been received from the straw poll taken by the Merchants' and Manufacturers' Association. Perhaps these additional returns, better than anything else, show how the opinion of the voters has crystalized in favor of the $2,000,000 issue.

Three days ago the returns showed 230 votes for the bonds and seven against. Last night over 300 answers had been received and of the additional returns not one vote is against the bond issue.

The vote now stands 301 for the bonds and 7 votes against.

. . .

1902: Now that the city owned its water works, it needed to keep it from flood-ing and destroying homes, business buildings, and infrastructure, which the river seemed to do with wintertime regularity. After terrible 1914 floods, city and county boosters joined local government officials and engineers in mounting an effort to stop major damages and protect their investment in the future. A special commit-tee of engineers devised a plan to control the runoff. The preservation of the Los Angeles and Long Beach harbors, where the Los Angeles River and the San Gabriel River, respectively, emptied into the Pacific Ocean, was of paramount importance in assuring future commerce for the Los Angeles region.

From Los Angeles County Board of Flood Control Engineers, "Report of the Board of Engineers to the Board of Supervisors" (typescript, 1915, pp. 6–15, Huntington Library, San Marino, CA).

INTRODUCTORY

For many years successive Boards of Supervisors have sought to give the county pro-tection against floods. The heavy flood damage of 1888 emphasized the need of ac-tion. In 1893 an unavailing effort was made to secure concerted action to control the San Gabriel River above El Monte. In 1898 a commission consisting of J. A. Street, C. T. Healey and H. Stafford were [sic] employed to investigate and report upon a suitable flood channel location and design for the San Gabriel River. Their report made, a period of comparatively dry years followed. Interest flagged and the need of adequate provision for controlling floods was forgotten.

FIGURE 10. Although it usually stayed within its banks in the summer, the Los Angeles River could flood vast areas in the winter.
Courtesy of the Los Angeles Public Library Photo Collection.

The high water of 1911 occasioned by heavy rainfalls in January, February and March awakened the people again to the fact that floods recur in Southern California. In answer to a general demand that action be taken, the Supervisors appointed Mr. Frank H. Olmsted, now a member of this Board, to investigate and report on San Gabriel River control. His report was filed and published October 1913. From that time on[,] the County authorities have been active, both in devising plans and as far as the legal limitations to their powers permitted[,] bettering flood conditions throughout the County. This has been impossible of wide accomplishment by reason of the narrow limits of their lawful powers. The Act which goes into effect on the 8th of August next enlarges these powers.

The flood control protection districts heretofore established in Los Angeles County, seven in number, have on the whole, been a disappointment and the protective works constructed have proved inadequate.

The Act of the Legislature now about to become effective provides a means whereby a general plan can be carried into effect. And protection of a permanent nature secured.

The flood control problem that confronted this Board involved studies of the physical characteristics of an area which includes precipitous mountains, detrital valleys and coastal plains, with rivers subject to enormous winter flood discharges through channels whose gradients rapidly change and whose courses, by the natural process of the upbringing of the valleys, gyrate through wide stretches of the most highly improved agricultural and horticultural districts in the United States. The engineering problems involved include flood prevention, flood protection, and harbor preservation. . . .

SAN FERNANDO DISTRICT

The San Fernando Valley, containing 112,000 acres of fertile valley land, is surrounded by high and precipitous mountains on its eastern side and by lower foothills and mountains on the north, west and south. The general trend of the valley floor is towards the southeast, with outlet some two miles in width near the town of Tropico. . . .

The eastern mountains are of crystalline rocks. The torrential streams erode these rocks and spread the debris over the eastern side of the valley in slopes of approximately fifty feet per mile. There have been thus built up great detrital deposits on the eastern side of the valley composed of coarse granite sands and boulders covering an area of about 30,000 acres possessed of great underground storage capacity, which act as a covered regulating reservoir. The floods being discharged on this pervious mass are absorbed in part and create an underground body of water[,] which sloping toward the narrow outlet of the valley there reappears on the surface as the constant, regulated flow of the Los Angeles River, which has furnished the water supply of practically the entire population of Los Angeles until the bringing of the waters of the Aqueduct. . . .

The Big and Little Tujungas [Rivers], now unrestrained, menace an area six miles in width and nine miles in length on the eastern side of the valley. Destructive floods make erratic excursions through orchards and garden tracts worth approximately $1,000.00 per acre. No lands within this district are safe under existing conditions. In the western portion of the valley broad sheets of water have spread over highways, orchards and town sites, causing great damage and inconvenience and creating conditions which demand remedy. . . .

The detailed report on the valley shows it to be the most advisable to carry the flood waters of the Tujunga through their westerly channel to the Los Angeles River, and those of the Pacoima in a southerly course from its canyon mouth past the county rock quarry at Pacoima to a junction with the main channel of the Tujungas.

In addition it is proposed to provide adequate conduits for the conveyance of the flood waters from the extreme northeast corner of the valley through to the Los Angeles River, and also from the western portion of the valley to the central depression of the valley south of Owensmouth. This will include a channel from Chatsworth Park and one from Zelzah. Rights of way would have to be obtained for this conduit as well as for a main channel of the Los Angeles River from a point west of Owensmouth through to its connection with the Tujungas. . . .

The conduit from north of the town of San Fernando through to the Los Angeles River would be of masonry, as well as the Zelzah conduit, and a portion of the Chatsworth conduit south of 12th Street, and the Los Angeles River Channel west of De Soto Avenue through the town of Owensmouth. The main channel of the Los Angeles River from De Soto Avenue to its junction with the Big Tujunga would not be lined unless future experience should demonstrate the need thereof. . . .

COASTAL PLAIN SOUTH AND EAST OF LOS ANGELES

The coastal plain south and east of Los Angeles extends inland from the Pacific Ocean to the Paso de Bartolo about twenty miles, and from Inglewood to the east county boundary between fifteen and twenty miles. It rises gradually from sea level to an elevation of about 250 feet. The gentle slope is broken only by the line of low hills of which Dominguez Hill and Signal Hill are the chief elevations.

The Los Angeles River from 1824 to 1889 flowed directly south from the City of Los Angeles to its present mouth at Long Beach. In 1889 it changed its course easterly through Vernon[,] rejoining its old channel near the County Farm. The Rio Hondo has followed fairly uniformly its present channel to a confluence with the Los Angeles near the County Farm. The San Gabriel after passing the Whittier Narrows has at various times emptied either into Alamitos Bay or joined the Los Angeles River via the Rio Hondo, or as in 1888 when it passed near Bouton Lake. The most vital requirement in the control of these three rivers is the protection of Los Angeles Harbor from the immense amount of silt which these rivers have brought down in time past and which they will continue to bring in increasing measure until properly controlled. This is true not only because Los Angeles Harbor is probably the greatest single asset of the County, but because the authority of the Federal Government in protecting navigable water is such that all efforts to control the rivers higher up must comply with whatever plans may be adopted by the Government for the protection of the harbor. . . .

From the City of Los Angeles, south to Dominguez, the Los Angeles River should be returned to the channel which it occupied prior to 1889. In general, it is proposed to provide a central trapezoidal channel sufficient for the ordinary flows with wide berme planted to cane and willows and rip-rap protection where needed. . . .

PUBLIC NECESSITY

The estimated cost of the complete works outlined in this report is $16,508,900. The loss which occurred in the flood of 1914 was over ten million dollars, or over sixty per cent of this amount. Destructive floods will occur in average intervals of less than five years.

The costs of rights of way are rapidly increasing. The value of menaced property and of consequent damages will advance with the improvement of the country.

Prompt relief from these floods is an urgent public necessity. Supine indifference to this menace is not in accordance with the customs of this community.

H. HAWGOOD, Chairman

CHAS. T. LEEDS

J. B. LIPPINCOTT

F. H. OLMSTED, Secretary

· · ·

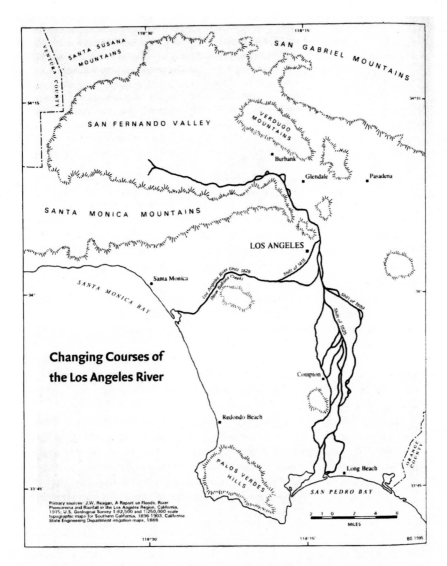

MAP 1. Some nineteenth-century Angelenos remembered (or learned from their elders) that the Los Angeles River once flowed westward from the site of the present-day Los Angeles Coliseum and emptied into Santa Monica Bay at Ballona Creek. In 1825 the river jumped its banks and headed south to the San Pedro Bay harbor. In this map, geographer Blake Gumprecht traces the several moves the river made before it was finally encased in concrete. Courtesy of Blake Gumprecht.

In the same year, public officials and boosters organized an effort to create a special agency encompassing most of Los Angeles County to finance and manage the flood control system. Over the next several decades, many more plans would be made and infrastructure created to protect an ever-increasing number of homes, stores, and other structures that sprouted on the landscapes of urban growth. Eventually the riverbed would be set in concrete in an attempt to fasten it in place and make it behave.

From "First Long Step Made Toward Flood Control" (*Los Angeles Times,* July 28, 1915).

"FIRST LONG STEP MADE TOWARD FLOOD CONTROL: COUNTY BOARD OF
ENGINEERS SUBMITS EXHAUSTIVE PLANS CALLING FOR FIVE YEARS'
WORK AT COST OF SIXTEEN AND A HALF MILLIONS—NEXT MOVE IS TO
FORM DISTRICT, VOTE BONDS, HIRE A BOSS AND START"

Estimating the cost of adequate flood control for Los Angeles County at $16,508,900, the Board of Engineers, Flood Control, submitted collective and individual reports to the Board of Supervisors yesterday, and the body was dissolved, after spending $100,000 in investigations and drafting plans.

The estimate includes an item of $1,827,000 for work in connection with the harbor. This expenditure will probably be borne by the government, thus reducing the county's estimated outlay to $14,681,900, or $5,000,000 in excess of the preliminary estimate, made shortly after the board was organized.

Further reductions in the county's outlay through State aid is expected. In this connection it is recommended that steps be immediately taken looking towards co-operation by the State and Federal governments in the work, which it is estimated will take about five years to complete. . . .

All five of the engineers agree that the diversion of flood waters from the harbor is the major desideratum of the whole plan, it being set forth in axiomlike form in the main report that the harbor is the county's greatest asset. In this connection the proposed visits [in] the coming month of both the Rivers and Harbors Committee of the United States House of Representatives and the Board of Engineers for Rivers and Harbors, War Department, is considered as recognition that the harbor is a government asset to be safeguarded.

THE NEXT STEP

Dissolution of the Board of Engineers, Flood Control, means simply that one unit of the great work of "removing the risk" from 215,300 acres of land, valued conservatively at more than $50,000,000, has been completed. The second step, under the terms of a bill passed by the last Legislature, at the solicitation of the Los Angeles County Flood Control Association, is to create a flood control district, issue bonds and appoint an engineer to supervise the work. To give the electorate an opportunity to study the subject, before initiatory steps are taken, the Board of Supervisors authorized the printing of the full text of the engineers' report in the following words: "At a meeting looking to relief from flood damage recently held in Topeka, Kan., it was estimated that flood damage in the State of Kansas during the present year, 1913, amounted to $15,000,000. The State of Kansas has an area of 82,158 square miles. Los Angeles County has 4067 square miles. If the relative economic interests are directly proportional to the amount of damage and inversely as to the area, then Los Angeles has an incentive about twenty times as great as that of Kansas to accomplish flood control."

In general, the plan of both the majority and minority of the Board of Engineers for adequate flood control contemplates, in the words of Mr. Reagan [a member of the board], "conservation, retardation, reforestation, spreading of the waters of some streams, diversion of those of others, and channel rectification and improvements." . . .

IN THE SAN FERNANDO

Spreading and assisting waters to percolate under-ground is proposed for the San Fernando Valley, with conveyance of the flood waters of the Tejungas through their westerly channel to the Los Angeles River, and those of the Pacoima in a southerly course from its canyon mouth past the county rock quarry at Pacoima in a junction with the main channel of the Tejungas. In addition it is proposed to provide adequate conduits for the conveyance of the flood waters from the extreme southeast corner of the valley through the Los Angeles River, and also from the western portion of the valley to the central depression of the valley south of Owensmouth. This will include a channel from Chatsworth Park and one from Zelzah, to cost $679,000 for structures and $80,000 for rights of way, including work at San Fernando and Wilson.

"A rapid increase in the population of the valley is expected," says the board's report. "The time is opportune for acquiring rights of way." . . .

Hundreds of other recommendations are made, affecting all parts of the county, and calculated to make all land area from the mountains to the sea immune from flood.

• • •

In the mid-1930s the U.S. Army Corps of Engineers assumed most of the responsibility for flood control work in the county. The major downpour in 1938 caused massive flooding in the area and spurred civic and business leaders, as well as federal and local officials and engineers, to search for a more permanent method of controlling the Los Angeles and other rivers to prevent future destruction and ensure continued urban growth. Lining the riverbed with concrete was the preferred method of the Army Corps of Engineers. Such a scheme was designed to speed floodwater to the ocean so that it would not rise over the river's banks and wreak havoc. Over the next several decades, about fifty-one miles of the Los Angeles River would be encased in concrete.

From U.S. Army Corps of Engineers, "Flood Control in the Los Angeles County Drainage Area" (May, 1938, pp. 1–4, held by Special Collections, Claremont Colleges Library, Claremont, CA).

FIGURE 11. Damage in North Hollywood as a result of the 1938 flood.
Courtesy of the Los Angeles Public Library Photo Collection.

The populous city of Los Angeles and its suburbs are situated on a fertile plain which is under a more dangerous flood menace than any similar region in the United States.

An unfavorable relation of topography, volume and occurrence of rainfall, and occupancy by a large city and numerous adjacent towns and settlements call for an extraordinary variety of design and construct in order to provide adequate flood protection. The topography is made up of mountains and ridges which border and traverse the land except on the ocean side. Drainage is provided by the Los Angeles River; its large tributary, the Rio Hondo; the San Gabriel River; and Ballona Creek, each fed by many branches, arroyos, and washes from mountain and ridge slopes. All these streams follow a general southerly direction on their course to the ocean. The rains are torrential, transforming the streams, normally dry or of little volume, into raging torrents which transport soil, gravel, and boulders, scouring their channels and flooding the low-lands. The impetus and fierceness of these floods can be likened to that of the discharge of a bursting dam. This was vividly illustrated by the New Year's Day flood of 1934, when flood-transported debris devastated the suburbs of Montrose and La Crescenta, and again by the flood of March 2, 1938, when destruction was general along the foothill area from San Bernardino to San Fernando. The combination of these factors, which affect or are affected by the floods, makes necessary regulation at many points by many kinds of structures for the achievement of adequate flood control.

Attention was first formally directed to the problem of flood control about 23 years ago, resulting in the formation of the Los Angeles County Flood Control District. However, instead of diminishing, the requirements for protection against flood have increased as the work has proceeded. One of the principal factors contributing to this increase is the increase in the rate of run-off, with its consequent increase in flood peaks. This manifestation is explained in the history of the growth of Los Angeles and its neighboring cities, with the increase in imperviousness which accompanies such growth through increase in roof and street areas. The flood control requirements are further augmented by increased land values, new residential districts, and the development of high-priced orchards. More specifically, the property valuation in the county is six times the valuation two decades ago.

The magnitude of the problem is made comprehensible by the fact that Los Angeles County has already spent sixty millions in the building of parts of the required protective works, and a plan is now contemplated which will aggregate seventy millions more. Even the size of these figures, however, cannot reveal the difficulty and diversity of the engineering problems involved. In addition to the need for curbing the flood waters and debris, matters are further complicated by the necessity of conserving as much as is possible of the discharging flood waters to replenish the ground water storage, heavily depleted in recent years, and on which the life of much of the region depends. . . .

Since the inauguration of work under an allotment of W.P.A. funds, the passage of the Flood Control Act of 1936 has placed the flood protection of the Los Angeles area under the category of a Definite Federal Project, and provides for the ultimate expenditure of federal funds not to exceed $70,000,000 for its completion, subject to approval of plans by the Chief of Engineers, on recommendation by the Board of Engineers for Rivers and Harbors.

The work to date has been done at points where flood danger was most imminent. In foothill areas, basins and dams have been built to trap water-borne debris and to check water traveling at high velocities; and channels have been constructed to control the water flowing from those debris basins. Below the foothills and on the coastal plain, various channels have been enlarged, straightened, and provided with bank protection, or inclosed in reinforced concrete channels. In low-lying areas, the drainage problem has been met by providing more efficient drainage into the ocean, or by the installation of pumping works, to raise the storm water to elevations where it will drain off.

Present and contemplated work is of a nature similar to that already accomplished, except that several large earth-filled dams will be constructed to form flood control basins. These will serve the triple purpose of reducing peak run-off, catching debris carried by the stream, and holding the water so that it can be released at a rate which will permit increased percolation into the streambed, thereby conserving much of the run-off which would otherwise waste into the ocean.

· · ·

MAP 2. Los Angeles receives water from several sources besides the Owens and Colorado Rivers appearing in this map of the major conveyances (the Los Angeles River is not included). One other major source is the State Water Project, which carries water through the California Aqueduct from Northern to Southern California, where some of it is emptied into the Colorado River Aqueduct headed toward Los Angeles and nearby communities.

Courtesy of the Metropolitan Water District of Southern California.

THE OWENS RIVER

Plans to control the flow of the Los Angeles River did not satisfy boosters for long. In fact city engineers immediately began to look for more water to support antici- pated growth. It was found about 250 miles away, in Inyo County. Engineers pro- posed building an aqueduct on, or in, the Owens River to bring it to Los Angeles. This rapidly became a major project for the city's progressives as a public effort to expand and manage a natural resource for the good of all city residents. Over the years, the progressives fought to protect this venture from those who sought to take advantage of it, and from those who claimed it had been a plan hatched in perdition. City officials desirous of acquiring patronage jobs and implicated in possible graft were often challenged; in the meantime, investors who had bought once-dry land saw their property values rise when the water arrived. And Los Angles' city limits expanded as communities and incorporated cities were annexed to it in order to obtain a dependable water source.

From Burt A. Heinly, "Municipal Progressiveness and the Los Angeles Aqueduct" (*The American City* 6 [April 1912]: 662).

In 1905 the city of Los Angeles voted to undertake the construction of the Owens River project. September 20, 1907, the first shovelful of earth was thrown in the exca- vation of the 240-mile aqueduct. Today sees the work 85 per cent completed in point of hardship and 79 per cent in point of distance. January 1, 1913, should find the floods of the Sierra watering the soil of the San Fernando Valley near the city's gates.

For 130 miles this water course of steel and concrete skirts the western edge of the Mojave Desert, then tunnels the Coast Range and enters the Pacific coastal plain, bringing not merely the certainty of a pure and copious domestic water supply, but tremendous possibilities of hydro-electric power development and the irrigation of 135,000 acres of dry land contiguous to the city. The history of the undertaking is a record of seven years of public unity in which no bickerings or party politics have been permitted to enter; the men to whom the city intrusted the enterprise have been left free to perform their duty to the best of their ability, knowing that Los Angeles believed in them—trusted them. The enterprise is a remarkable one, even if it were not one of the most daring engineering feats ever attempted. With the exception of one small contract amounting to less than three per cent of the whole, *all the work has been done by the city itself. The task is being completed nearly a year in advance of the time for which it was promised and well within the $24,500,000 issue of bonds voted for the purpose* [italics in original]. This statement is based on the percentage of the mileage now finished and the cost of work to date.

For the past three years the progress has been at the rate of a little more than fifty miles annually. The army of 4,000 men equipped with power shovels and other forms of the most powerful and modern forms of excavating machinery have worked si- multaneously from fifty camps, wherein water, food and all other necessities of life have had to be carried into the desert for them. . . .

One feature of the work to which little or no publicity has been given is that the municipality is dividing with labor the profits resulting from labor's intense application to its task. In addition to a daily wage, labor is paid *pro rata* whenever a certain rate of progress is exceeded in a ten-day interval. Along the aqueduct the man with the shovel or 'barrow or trowel has learned to measure his task, not by the eight-hour day, but by how much it is possible for him to accomplish in that period. To this community of interest between the municipality and its copartner, labor, is to be traced much of the low cost and unusual speed with which the enterprise is being advanced towards completion. . . .

With all the available power fully developed, and with a ready market for her water to irrigators and domestic consumers, Los Angeles estimates that for a total expenditure of $31,500,000 she will have a going concern that will pay her a net annual revenue of $4,425,000, which is the equivalent of 5 per cent interest on $88,500,000.

· · ·

Aqueduct plans were initially kept secret to prevent the escalation of the price of water rights and land values in the Owens Valley; the project was finally made public knowledge in 1905. Soon thereafter, it was revealed that a syndicate of wealthy businessmen who purchased property in the San Fernando Valley had been tipped off about the aqueduct project ahead of time. The syndicate they formed was able to buy up thousands of acres of land at pre-aqueduct prices, very near to where the aqueduct would in fact terminate.

From *Articles of Incorporation of the San Fernando Mission Land Company* (December 3, 1904, Seaver Center for Western History Research, Los Angeles County Museum of Natural History).

KNOW ALL MEN BY THESE PRESENTS:

That we, the undersigned, a majority of whom are citizens and residents of the State of California, have this day voluntarily associated ourselves together for the purpose of forming a corporation under the laws of the State of California.

AND WE HEREBY CERTIFY:

FIRST—That the name of said corporation shall be the San Fernando Mission Land Company.

SECOND—That the purposes for which it is formed are to buy and sell land and water, to subdivide land into farm or town lots and sell same, to develop water for domestic or irrigating purposes and sell same, to form stock corporations for the development, use and sale of water, to buy stock of any corporation where water can be obtained for the use of land and to do a general land and water business in buying and selling same, to incur bonded or other indebtedness, to execute Deeds, Mortgages, Powers of Attorney or other instruments, to facilitate the purchase and sale of land and water, all of which business is to be done for profit.

FIGURE 12. Harvesting grain on the Van Nuys Lankershim Ranch in the San Fernando Valley circa 1905.
From the C. C. Pierce Collection of Photographs, photCL Pierce 05519, courtesy of The Huntington Library, San Marino, California.

THIRD—That the place where the principal business of said Corporation is to be transacted is _____ Los Angeles, California.

FOURTH—That the term for which said Corporation is to exist is fifty years, from and after the date of its incorporation.

FIFTH—That the number of Directors or Trustees of said Corporation shall be seven and that the names and residences of the Directors or Trustees, who are appointed for the first year, and to serve until the election and qualification of such officers, are as follows to-wit:

Name	Whose Residence is at
H. E. Huntington	Los Angeles, Cal.
E. H. Harriman	New York
H. G. Otis	Los Angeles, Cal.
W. G. Kerckhoff	Los Angeles, Cal.
J. F. Sartori	Los Angeles, Cal.
L. C. Brand	Los Angeles, Cal.
E. T. Earl	Los Angeles, Cal.

FIGURES 13, 14, 15, AND 16. Members of the San Fernando Mission Land Company included (*clockwise from top left*) Henry E. Huntington, Harrison G. Otis, Joseph Sartori, and Edwin T. Earl.

Photo of Huntington from the Henry E. Huntington Collection, HEH 61/2/7 (10), courtesy of The Huntington Library, San Marino, California. Photo of Otis courtesy of the University of Southern California, on behalf of the USC Libraries. Photo of Sartori courtesy of the Los Angeles Public Library Photo Collection. Photo of Earl from the C. C. Pierce Collection of Photographs, photCL Pierce 08609, courtesy of The Huntington Library, San Marino, California.

SIXTH—That the amount of the Capital Stock of said Corporation is One Million Dollars, and the number of Shares into which it is divided is Ten Thousand of the par value of One Hundred Dollars, each.

. . .

. . .

Although the syndicate had purchased the San Fernando Valley property long before the Owens River project was announced, the timing of this revelation spurred some opponents to charge that the entire project was *created* by the syndicate to reap the profits from a publicly financed venture. This conspiracy thesis became a much-believed tenet of local history over the years and was a central feature in the famed motion picture *Chinatown*. In all likelihood the syndicate was probably informed of the planned purchase by Moses Sherman, a city water commissioner and an associate of some of the syndicate leaders. Below is an early description of the conspiracy by an opponent who was criticized by project proponents for frequently stretching the truth.

From W. T. Spilman, *The Conspiracy: An Exposure of the Owens River Water and San Fernando Land Frauds* ([Los Angeles: Alembic Club, 1912], 57–60, Huntington Library, San Marino, CA).

The summer of 1903 was the time of the City's first artificial shortage of water. It was also the second year of constructing the fake tunnel. The newspapers paraded this alleged shortage of water and the fake tunnel to the people throughout the season without there being any move or sign of an exposure of these deceptions. Book 1919, Page 153, Record of Deeds, Los Angeles County, shows that in the autumn of this same year Mr. L. C. Brand took a three-years' option in trust of date, October 13, 1903, on the Porter Land and Water Company's great ranch at a price of $35 per acre.

This trust has since been terminated by incorporating it under the name of the San Fernando Mission Land Company with:

1. H. G. Otis, chief owner and general manager of the Los Angeles Times.
2. E. T. Earl, owner of the Los Angeles Express and The Tribune
3. L. C. Brand, largely interested in the Los Angeles Times.
4. E. H. Harriman, deceased, and late president of the Southern Pacific, whose railroad interests are now represented by Judge Robert S. Lovett.
5. W. H. *[sic]* Kerckhoff, president of the Pacific Light & Power Company of Los Angeles.
6. H. E. Huntington, president of the Los Angeles Railway Company of Los Angeles.
7. J. F. Sartori, president of the Security Savings Bank of Los Angeles, California, as directors.

Mr. M. H. Sherman, vice president of the Los Angeles Pacific Railroad[,] was a stockholder in this land company and also a member of the Board of Water Commissioners at the time of taking this option.

This princely estate is better known as the George K. Porter Ranch; and it has an area upwards of twenty-eight square miles. It is situated in the upper end of the San Fernando valley, immediately at the point where the Owens River aqueduct terminates. This vast body of land is of little value in its natural dry state, but with water it stands unexcelled as an orange and lemon belt in Southern California. It is fertile and practically frostless.

Now the question is, did these gentlemen have knowledge of the Owens River project at the time they took that extraordinary long-period option[,] and have they been secretly guiding the workings of this great scheme; or was it due to the kindness of the fates that Messrs. Otis and Earl with their wealthy associates fell into this great land bargain? Or did they unwittingly take a three-year's option on this land with only a blind hope that something would occur to make it valuable?

The San Fernando valley contains 112,640 acres[,] and Messrs. Otis and Sherman with other wealthy gentlemen have, since the first purchase, bought at about the same price practically all of the remainder of the valley, except a small tract in the vicinity of Burbank that was subdivided a number of years ago.

(QUOTATION NO. 34)

In a booklet issued in 1910–1911 by the Los Angeles Suburban Homes Company, a corporation composed of H. G. Otis and his wealthy associates as owners and developers, they say:

> "At the Northerly Gateway of Los Angeles."
> "And this beckoning gate is now ajar."
> "View of portion of the aqueduct which will bring
> Owens River water to a vast reservoir adjacent to these lands."

MORE ABOUT THE WATER SUPPLY

"There will be created a great reservoir-lake for the storage of the pure fluid coming down from the base of the snow-clad Sierras, the reservoir having already been selected in the foothills hard by the tract of land here described; and to reach the city the Owens River water must traverse the San Fernando valley.

"Purchasers of land here will share equitably in the primary right that will undoubtedly be accorded the residents of the San Fernando valley to be the first consumers beyond the City limits to share in the surplus water that will be brought down by the great aqueduct. They will thus enjoy greater advantages than can come to any other section, besides such special advantages as may result from contiguity.

"Surveys and plans of distribution are already being made for covering all the available portions of the great valley with the immense surplus of the Owens River water which it is confidently believed will be available when the capacious conduit is in full operation less than three years hence."

COMMENT

This alluring advertisement [above] is put out by the corporation composed of Mr. H. G. Otis and his wealthy associates and it only applies to the Van Nuys–Lankershim lands which are situated in the lower half of the San Fernando valley, the upper portion not having as yet been put upon the market.

By this class of advertising[,] which virtually promises the Owens River water for the irrigation of this land[,] they have boosted its price from about $35 to $400 per acre,

FIGURE 17. Los Angeles political reform activist Dr. John Randolph Haynes, circa 1930. Courtesy of the John Randolph Haynes and Dora Haynes Foundation.

FIGURE 18. Novelist and political activist Upton Sinclair in 1934. Courtesy of the Los Angeles Public Library Photo Collection.

making their profit more than tenfold. Thus they reap a golden harvest while the people of the City of Los Angeles pay the bills.

The lower half of the valley is not nearly as valuable as the upper half will be when supplied with water[;] nevertheless, even at the prices they are selling the low lands show what colossal fortunes these gentlemen are making out of this scheme and that without any regard as to the welfare of either the city or the poor people who buy these lands of them.

. . .

The idea that conspiracy explained the entire aqueduct project—a belief held by many at the time—was doubted by Dr. John Randolph Haynes, a wealthy physician and political activist in Los Angeles. In the following letter, Haynes informs his friend, the novelist and social critic Upton Sinclair, that he was invited to join the syndicate early on but declined because of the lack of available water.

From Dr. John Randolph Haynes to Upton Sinclair (August 13, 1919, Box 19, Upton Sinclair Papers, courtesy of the Lilly Library, Indiana University, Bloomington, IN).

August 13, 1919

My dear Mr. Sinclair:

With reference to the building of the Owens River Aqueduct there are a number of stories in circulation which from my personal knowledge I know to be without foundation. It has been charged, for example, that the "drouth" in the years immediately proceeding the undertaking was fictitious in character, gotten up by the promoters of the project to persuade people to take that action; that the purchasers of the Porter Ranch bought the property with the idea of getting the city to build the Aqueduct and of thereby reaping enormous profits; and that the work of construction on the Aqueduct was poorly and uneconomically done.

Regarding the "drouth" fiction, I remember very well the dry years because I and many others felt that it might mean an end to the city's growth. I remember that I refused to loan money on certain city properties for that reason. I was then living at 945 South Figueroa St., and the property adjoining me—on the corner—consisting of one hundred and eight (108) feet frontage was offered to me for $4500. For the reason I mentioned I declined to buy. That property today[,] although located a little beyond the present business district, is worth at a conservative estimate $130,000. There was much talk of bringing water from the so called "Bouton Wells," from Mojave River, of sinking wells in the Tujunga Wash, etc., but all one after another were given up either because of engineering difficulties or because of the doubt of being able to secure legal title to the water rights; and because none of these projects assured anything like an adequate supply. The Owens River idea met with approval because the supply was large; and there was no question of prior claims from other communities since it was at that time running to waste in a dead salt sea, Owens Lake.

I know that the syndicate organized to buy the Porter ranch had no thought at the time of securing Owens River water because I was asked to join and to take a one-tenth interest. I talked with Otis and the others who urged me to join. Although many considerations were advanced in favor of the purchase, nothing was said about the Owens River as a source of water supply. I turned the matter down because I did not feel sure of the safety of the investment. Of course, after the ranch was purchased and the Owens River project was later put forward, these men boosted it. I think that the owners of the Porter Ranch should have been compelled to pay a bigger bonus than they did to get the Aqueduct water, possibly two or three hundred dollars an acre; but I am sure that there is no truth in the charge that they bought the ranch with the idea that they could persuade the city to bring down the Owens River water.

With reference to the construction of the Aqueduct[,] there were of course, some mistakes made, only one of a serious character however. This involved a loss of possibly forty, or fifty[,] thousand dollars. On the whole, however, according to the opinion of experts from all parts of the world, it is a wonderfully good piece of work, economically built. According to Edgerton, a member of the State Railway Commission, and a very honest man, it is one of the best and cheapest engineering tasks ever performed. It is a tribute to the enterprise of the people of Los Angeles and a magnificent monument to Wm. Mulholland the engineer.

I do not believe that Mulholland was as considerate of the interests of the workers on the aqueduct in some respects as he ought to have been[,] but I believe that he did drive the best bargain for the city that he could in all matters.

It is difficult for me to be patient sometimes with certain socialistic factions which on general principles are perpetually clamoring for public ownership of the industries and yet[,] whenever we do make a magnificent success of publicly owned enterprises, try to bark their heads off concerning minor defects and even resort to the circulation of reports false and misleading.

Even if their stories were true concerning the aqueduct, which they are not, in the interest of the socialist movement they should put in their time telling of the wonderful benefits the aqueduct is giving us instead of harping about the mistakes made in constructing it.

As a matter of fact the city today would be in an awful fix if the Owens River Canal had not been built. As it is, the city is growing and will continue to grow by leaps and bounds. The president of the Goodyear Company has publically stated that the water supply of Los Angeles and the cheap electrical power were the determining reasons for locating their immense plant at Los Angeles rather than at San Diego, San Francisco or other cities which were considered. And this is but the beginning. Los Angeles will soon be a city of a million people.

Apologizing to you for the delay in answering your letter, which was due, as I wrote you, to illness, I remain with best regards

Yours very truly,
John R. Haynes

. . .

Some engineers and former city officials also came under fierce criticism for their roles in the project. J. B. Lippincott, an engineer with the U.S. Reclamation Service, worked simultaneously for the City of Los Angeles as a consulting engineer while employed by the federal government. This was a clear conflict of interest, made all the more apparent when the Reclamation Service, which had initially considered developing the project, instead handed it over to Los Angeles. Former Los Angeles mayor Fred Eaton, who first suggested the Owens River as a possible source of freshwater for L.A., tried to personally cash in by selling land (especially for a reservoir site) that he had purchased in the Owens Valley when acting on behalf of the city. Eaton offered these holdings for sale to Los Angeles at an inflated price, offerings that his no doubt flabbergasted colleagues in the city rebuffed.

From J. B. Lippincott to Fernand Lungren (September 15, 1905, Box 1, Fernand Lungren Papers, Huntington Library, San Marino, CA).

September 15, 1905
Mr. Fernand Lungren
201 E. Ave. 41
Los Angeles, Cal.

Dear Sir:

In compliance with our conversation of yesterday, I am writing you concerning the Owens Valley situation.

The water supply of Southern California in general, and particularly around Los Angeles, is failing. This section has far outgrown the point where it can sustain itself on the surface streams, and has started an invasion on the underground water supplies by pumping in practically every part of Southern California. These extractions from the underground waters have caused a most serious dropping of the water plane. The City of Los Angeles has avoided a water famine on several occasions of late by appeals to the people through the press to cease using water during certain periods of drouth and hot weather. . . .

The City for a period now of a year has been quietly investigating other sources of water supply. Mr. Fred Eaton, member of the American Society of Civil Engineers, has been Mayor of the City of Los Angeles, City Engineer, and repeatedly Consulting Engineer for the town. Eaton and I, previous to my accepting a commission with the Reclamation Service, were probably among the principal ones who assisted in bringing about a municipal ownership of our water works, about five years ago. Today this system is owned by the City of Los Angeles. In the year 1904 this water works paid all operating and maintenance charges, provided interest and sinking funds for the bonds and depreciation of the plant and netted to the City as profit $640,000 after having reduced the water rate fully 10% upon the assumption of the plant by the municipality. We now have about the cheapest water rate in California. . . .

Mr. Eaton has lived in Owens Valley and he has called the attention of the City of Los Angeles to the possibility of bringing Owens River to that town. The work of doing this will be probably one of the most monumental and gigantic undertakings for a municipal water system that has ever been attempted on this continent. It involves an expenditure ultimately of about $25,000,000, and the construction of a concrete conduit that will be 209 miles in length, with an internal diameter of about 15 feet. The Owens River drains the easterly face of the Sierra Nevada Mountains for a distance of about 100 miles, including the region in the neighborhood of Mt. Whitney, Mt. Dana, and other snow-covered peaks. . . .

Yours very truly,

J. B. Lippincott

. . .

The Owens River Aqueduct project became a hot political issue in the 1911 municipal election in Los Angeles. Candidates running on the Socialist Party platform pledged to complete the project, while condemning both land syndicate "exploiters" and the progressive city administration for the parts they played in the project. In the primary election, Socialist mayoral candidate Job Harriman came very close to winning the election, an outcome that probably would have changed the course of water history in Los Angeles.

From "Municipal Platform: Socialist Party of Los Angeles" (August 6, 1911, Box 57, John R. Haynes Papers, Department of Special Collections, Charles E. Young Research Library, UCLA).

OUR WATER SUPPLY

We favor the hastening [of] the work of completing the Owens River Aqueduct, for which the people of Los Angeles have devoted $23,000,000 under the belief that the water and the electric energy to be derived therefrom was to be delivered to the people, and used for their benefit.

We demand that this electric power be held by the people to their use and not delivered now or at any time in the future to any corporation of avaricious and exploiting capitalists.

We pledge ourselves to take immediate steps towards bringing the Owens River water to Los Angeles. We view with utmost abhorrence plans which have been secretly carried out for years and which, if allowed to be consummated, would result in flowing the waters of the aqueduct upon lands held by some of the most infamous exploiters of land and labor in America.

We condemn the present city administration for permitting and causing the workers on the aqueduct to be fed upon and forced to eat a short allowance of spoiled and unhealthful food in order to increase the profit of private contractors, and we pledge ourselves to remedy this evil if placed in power.

• • •

In 1912, critics of the aqueduct convinced the Los Angeles City Council to appoint an investigative body to examine all aspects of the project. In the following passage contained in the board's final report (a report that filled seven volumes), former mayor Fred Eaton is singled out for special criticism for his self-interest.

From Ingle Carpenter report on Fred Eaton, in Los Angeles Aqueduct Investigation Board, *Report of the Aqueduct Investigation Board to the City Council of Los Angeles* (7 vols., 1912, 1:103–109).

TO THE AQUEDUCT INVESTIGATION BOARD,

Gentlemen:

Upon your request for a brief opinion on the law relative to the evidence taken before your Board as to the purchase, through Mr. Fred Eaton[,] of the land and water rights during the year 1906, I give you the following brief opinion:

The evidence shows that Mr. Mulholland, at that time superintendent of the city water works, Mr. W. B. Mathews, at that time City Attorney, and Fred Eaton were

FIGURE 19. Fred Eaton, mayor of Los Angeles, 1898–1900.
Courtesy of the Seaver Center for Western History Research, Los Angeles County Museum of Natural History.

jointly interested in securing for the city the important lands and water rights in Owens River Valley in the fall of 1904 and in 1906.

That Mr. Mulholland had made a survey for the proposed aqueduct, and that careful surveys are continued during the period referred to, in which he had out-lined the probable course of the aqueduct and the lands that would be necessary for the city to acquire.

That Mr. Mathews had been equally diligent in attending to the legal matters involved and in drawing up the necessary options to be taken upon the property that the city proposed to acquire. That it was necessary that the acquiring of this property should be concluded in the shape of options before the public in that locality became aware of the need of the city, and raised their prices. That Mr. Fred Eaton had resided in that locality and knew the various residents whose property it was desirable to purchase, and that he had been instrumental in bringing to Mr. Mulholland's attention the possibilities of that section, for water purposes.

That Mr. Eaton at that time had no interest in any of these lands proposed to be acquired for the city, and had no options and no negotiations for options of any sort at that time.

That it seemed necessary to Mr. Mulholland and Mr. Mathews that some one should act for the city in order to assume to negotiate for the lands and to take the title in his own name, until all the lands were acquired. That it appeared to the best interest of the city that Mr. Fred Eaton should be the one to act in that capacity.

Under these conditions, the evidence shows that Mr. Eaton, under the direction of Mr. Mulholland as to what were the necessary and important lands to be acquired, and under the legal direction of Mr. Mathews, who drafted the necessary options for the signatures of the important land-holders, went into the valley and for the first and most important option secured the option from the Rickey Land and Cattle Company which covered what appeared to be the most important land required for the aqueduct undertaking.

The letters during this period, written by Mr. Eaton to Mr. Mathews, show that the first option secured was on this land on March 22nd, 1905, and that Messrs. Eaton, Mathews, and Mulholland were working jointly to secure the same. Further letters at this time show the continuance of this arrangement, and there is nothing to show that Mr. Eaton was working at all independently or in any other capacity than that of representing the city, sub-rosa, in these undertakings. In the letter of April 6, 1905, Mr. Eaton writes Mr. Mathews that he has retained a local attorney, Ben Yandell, to attend to his work while he was absent, and the disbursements from the Water Revenue Fund show that this retainer was with the City of Los Angeles.

The minutes of the Board of Water Commissioners of May 22, 1905, show that the written proposal to sell the city certain lands, by Mr. Eaton, which lands are referred to and are the lands included in the first important option secured by Mr. Eaton, is accepted by a resolution of the Board which provides that Mr. Eaton will assign and transfer to the Board all options and contracts held by him.

It is further to be considered that the evidence shows that there was no written proposal before the board at that time, as the only written proposal made by Mr. Eaton was written a day later than the meeting of the Board, and was mailed at Carson City, Nevada.

It can but be concluded from this evidence that the only proposition before the board was the understanding under which Messrs. Mulholland, Mathews and Eaton seemed to have worked, which was that Mr. Eaton, in whose name these properties were to be taken for the benefit of the city, should transfer same by informal sale or transfer upon this resolution of the Board.

On June 6, 1905, the first payment on the property under the option appears to have been made, and this was made by Mr. Fay, President of the Water Board, at San Francisco[,] and $50,000 was paid over by him to the President of the Rickey Land and Cattle Company, and consisted of money belonging to the City of Los Angeles.

It appears from the evidence that about this time Mr. Eaton secured from the Rickey Land and Cattle Company a second option or agreement of sale, specifying only part of the property included in the original option, but taking another agreement or option for the balance provided for in the first option.

The minutes of the Water Commissioners of June 6, 1905, show an agreement made on that date between the City of Los Angeles and Mr. Eaton for the purchase of certain land which formed a part of the original option which Mr. Eaton had secured as already referred to. This agreement was made several days after Mr. Fay had paid the $50,000 on account of the purchase of the land and which he had paid direct to the president of the Rickey Land and Cattle Company.

It appears from the evidence that only a part of the lands in the original option which the resolution referred to seemed to require should be assigned and transferred to the Board of Water Commissioners, were included in this agreement of sale of June 6, 1905. It also appears from the testimony of Mr. Mulholland and Mr. Mathews that after Mr. Fay had paid the $50,000 upon the purchase of the property, the option or agreement on which stood in the name of Mr. Eaton, that Mr. Eaton came to Los Angeles and that Mr. Mulholland and Mr. Mathews arranged for this purchase or transfer[,] and at this point Mr. Eaton held up all the land and property in the option that he could; and that the property which the city finally secured by this agreement of June 6, 1905, was only a part of the property under the original option secured as has been stated.

The evidence of both Mr. Mulholland and Mr. Mathews shows that Mr. Eaton's attitude was unexpected, and was not in accordance with any arrangement that they may have had, and that for two days they fought at swords' points in securing from Mr. Eaton the property needed for the aqueduct. This, also, notwithstanding the fact that in the securing of the option Mr. Mathews and Mr. Mulholland had performed as important, if not more important, services than Mr. Eaton, and that the city had paid the $50,000 which had been paid upon the option, and that the necessity of Mr. Eaton in the deal was only for the use of his name to forestall public knowledge in that locality.

It appears that the property which Mr. Eaton retained from the original option and refused to transfer to the city, although the resolution of the Board had contemplated an assignment or transfer of all options and contracts, including five thousand head of cattle, all buildings and equipment of the ranch and one hundred head of horses and mules, a rebate to be returned to the holder of the option of $8.00 per acre upon unpatented land which Mr. Eaton calculated at from 5,000 to 17,000 acres, and approximately about one-half of the total acreage of the land included in the original option.

It appears also from the testimony that the city has since been obliged to buy a considerable part of this land, and that in order to carry out the proposed plans as to the Long Valley Reservoir a very large portion of this land now held by Mr. Eaton will have to be purchased; and while the data as to the exact value of the properties that Mr. Eaton retained is not at hand, still placing an approximate value upon the cattle and other properties, and the rebate, the further purchase he made for the city and the value which he has stated that he holds the balance of the required land at, would approximate upwards of three-quarters of a million dollars.

Taking in conjunction the evidence upon other real estate transactions subsequent to that time, when, upon his own request, Mr. Eaton was receiving $10 per day from the city as shown by the minutes of the Board of Water Commissioners, and the expenditures from the Water Revenue Fund, which evidence is before the Board, and which shows that he was receiving commissions during such period, aside from his salary, and that he made approximately $10,000 over and above any agreement on transactions involving $60,000, which, according to his agreement with the Water Board were purchased for a stipulated consideration, as shown in the minutes of said Board on June 6, 1905, I would conclude that any further evidence that might be secured relative to the option of the Rickey Land and Cattle Company with Mr. Eaton would substantiate the facts already stated.

Inasmuch as all members of the Board of Water Commissioners who have given any testimony have stated that their understanding was that Mr. Eaton should assign and transfer the option received by him, retaining as a commission the cattle referred to, and inasmuch as the Original First Annual Report of the Los Angeles Aqueduct, in referring to the inception of the idea, shows a misunderstanding on the part of the Board as to the real situation at that time as to the options, I can but conclude that Mr. Eaton, was, at the time he secured that option, working in the employment of the city under arrangements that he had with Mr. Mathews and Mr. Mulholland, and that the placing of the property in the name of Mr. Eaton was purely that he should act as trustee for the city in holding that option for the city's use and benefit, and that it was generally understood by the Board of Water Commissioners and by Mr. Mulholland and Mr. Mathews that Mr. Eaton should so act, and that he continued in that relation to the city until having actually secured the option in his name and the city having paid thereupon the sum of $50,000, when he arbitrarily insisted upon dealing with the city, claiming that he was the real owner of the option, and requiring the city to meet his terms; but that the Water Board were not informed of his change of front, and that the city was not getting the whole of the option.

This conclusion is fortified by the fact that it has been testified by Mr. Mathews and Mr. Mulholland and that it was necessary that the knowledge that the city was purchasing lands should be kept from the public in that locality and therefore at that time it was unwise to force Mr. Eaton, through the courts, to acknowledge his position as trustee, only, in the holding of these options.

The situation would lead to no other conclusion but that Mr. Eaton, in assuming to take the option from the Rickey Land and Cattle Company, upon which the city had paid $50,000 while it stood in his name, had voluntarily assumed to act as trustee for the reasons already stated; and all the evidence seems to prove conclusively that such was his position in carrying through this land option and purchase.

The evidence also seems conclusive, both from the report of the Water Board and from the testimony of the former members thereof, that they were not informed that Mr. Eaton had held up this larger part of the property included under the option, and the efforts of Mr. Eaton in securing the second option or contract of sale from the Rickey Land and Cattle Company, carrying with it a side agreement for the balance of the property not shown to the water board, would force us to this conclusion.

Mr. Eaton therefore held the property in his name and under the later contract of sale, as a resulting trust, to which the city is a beneficiary.

While the statute of limitations of the State of California will run against a resulting trust, it can only be applied as a defense on the part of Mr. Eaton after the Water

Board had received definite knowledge that he had repudiated his trust, and that he claimed to hold the property individually and for his own benefit.

The burden will be upon him to show as a defense, should he be sued as a trustee for the return of this property, that he gave notice direct to the Water Board that he repudiated his trust; inasmuch as the testimony shows that he secured the additional, otherwise unnecessary contract of sale and undisclosed side agreement, he will also have to explain why such was obtained, unless it was to keep from the Water Board, which represented the city, any knowledge that he had repudiated his trust.

. . .

The Aqueduct Investigation Board split apart as its Socialist and non-Socialist members disagreed on methods and conclusions. The board majority, two of the three being Socialists, finally adopted several resolutions presented to the Los Angeles City Council. The resolutions implicated Fred Eaton and city officials in the project, but the council declined to act upon or approve them.

From Charles E. Warner (chairman, Aqueduct Investigation Board, City of Los Angeles) to Los Angeles City Council (August 22, 1912, Box B-1978, Los Angeles City Records Center).

LOS ANGELES, CAL., AUGUST 22, 1912.

WHEREAS, official records, various correspondence in the files of Aqueduct Department, and the testimony of various witnesses who appeared before the People's Aqueduct Investigation Board, seem to indicate that the properties described in the original options on Owens River Valley lands, secured in the name of Fred Eaton previous to May 22, 1905, and, in some instances, subsequent to that date, were really held by said Eaton as Agent and Trustee for the City, and not of his own right; and,

WHEREAS, this Board submitted these testimonies to Ingle Carpenter, Examiner for this Board, and an opinion has been rendered to the effect that these testimonies support the view that said Eaton acted as Agent and Trustee for the City, as aforesaid; and,

WHEREAS, in the transfer to the City of the properties secured by said Eaton as aforesaid, he retained, as his own, land and other properties of great value, which as, Agent and Trustee as aforesaid, the said testimonies indicate he should have transferred to the city; and,

WHEREAS, records and other evidence indicate that certain of the properties retained by said Eaton were purchased afterwards by the City for a large consideration; and,

WHEREAS, it appears from the records and testimonies that certain of the lands secured as aforesaid by Fred Eaton, and retained by him, are believed to be essential to the Aqueduct Enterprise, and its complete development, and will have to be purchased by the City, in the event they are essential to said Project, should said Agency and Trusteeship of said Eaton not be established by due process of law; and,

WHEREAS, W. B. Mathews, Attorney; William Mulholland, Superintendent; John J. Fay Jr., President, and J. M. Elliott, member of the Water Board of the City of Los Angeles, were intimately associated with the conduct of the securing of said options by said Eaton;

NOW, THEREFORE, BE IT RESOLVED, That the People's Aqueduct Investigation Board recommend to the City Council that legal proceedings be instituted on behalf of the City against all of the persons above named, in order that the Agency and Trusteeship of said Eaton may be established, and that a complete accounting be required from each and every of said parties; and for such other and further relief as may be deemed just and right under all of the evidence;

AND BE IT FURTHER RESOLVED, That the Secretary of this Board be instructed to transmit a copy of these resolutions to the City Council, and to each of the daily papers of the City of Los Angeles.

I hereby certify that the above and foregoing is a true copy of the resolutions passed by this Board at its meeting this 22nd day of August, 1912.

[Signed] Aqueduct Investigation Board Secretary

. . .

Completed on time and under budget in 1913, the Los Angeles Aqueduct was one of the major water-supply projects of its time. Grand celebrations in Los Angeles and the San Fernando Valley (see the cover photograph) lasted two days and included the formal opening of the Los Angeles Museum of History, Science and Art (now the Natural History Museum of Los Angeles County) in Exposition Park.

. . .

With more growth came more thirst. And while the Los Angeles Aqueduct was successful, Los Angeles eventually needed more water and decided to return to the Owens Valley. Residents of the latter complained about this water imperialism and fought back with several bombings of the aqueduct. One critic was the sister of two of the leaders of valley residents, the Watterson brothers, who owned a bank in Bishop that failed during the turmoil and who were convicted of embezzlement. In this letter to novelist Mary Austin, who had lived in the Owens Valley, Elsie Watterson explained her views.

From Elsie Watterson to Mary Austin (April 4, 1928, AU5166, Mary H. Austin Papers, Huntington Library, San Marino, CA).

My dear Mrs. Austin—

If you have read the California papers—particularly those of Los Angeles—any time within the past eight months you undoubtedly know of the dreadful disaster that has overtaken Owens Valley and especially our family, in the failure of the Inyo County banks, for which my brothers, Wilfred and Mark, are at present in San Quentin.

FIGURE 20. Owens River water enters the aqueduct, 1913.
Courtesy of the Los Angeles Public Library Photo Collection.

FIGURE 21. Crowds at the 1913 celebration of Owens River water finding its way to Los Angeles. From the C. C. Pierce Collection of Photographs, photCL Pierce 06844, courtesy of The Huntington Library, San Marino, California.

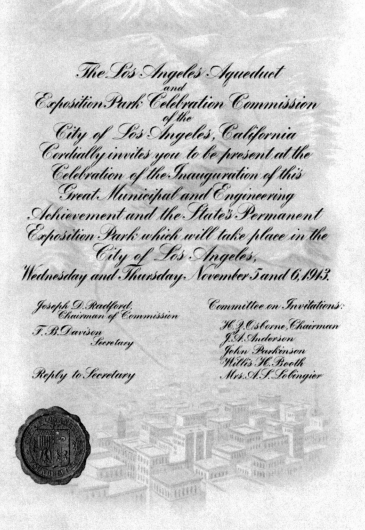

The Los Angeles Aqueduct
and
Exposition Park Celebration Commission
of the
City of Los Angeles, California
Cordially invites you to be present at the
Celebration of the Inauguration of this
Great Municipal and Engineering
Achievement and the State's Permanent
Exposition Park which will take place in the
City of Los Angeles,
Wednesday and Thursday November 5 and 6, 1913.

Joseph D. Radford,
Chairman of Commission

T. B. Davison
Secretary

Reply to Secretary

Committee on Invitations:

H. J. Osborne, Chairman
J. A. Anderson
John Parkinson
Willis H. Booth
Mrs. A. S. Lobingier

FIGURE 22. Invitation to the Owens River Aqueduct completion ceremonies in Exposition Park, 1913.
Courtesy of the Seaver Center for Western History Research, Los Angeles County Museum of Natural History.

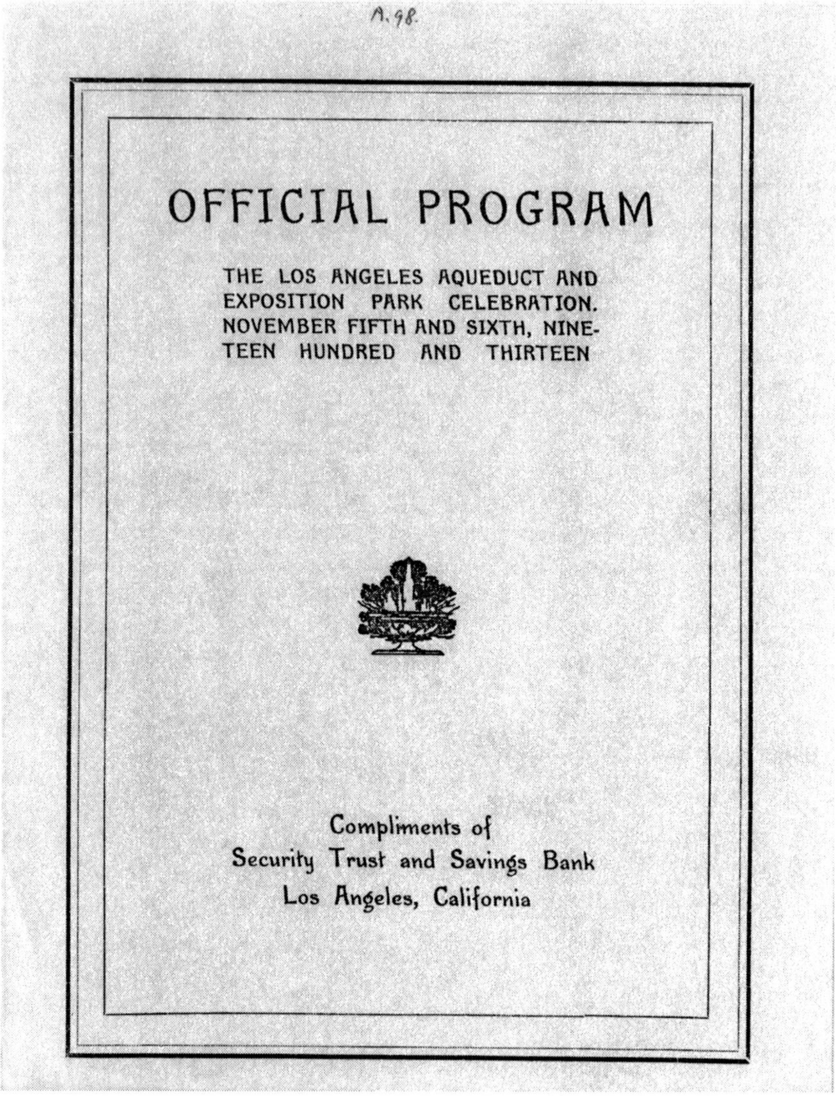

OFFICIAL PROGRAM

THE LOS ANGELES AQUEDUCT AND EXPOSITION PARK CELEBRATION. NOVEMBER FIFTH AND SIXTH, NINE-TEEN HUNDRED AND THIRTEEN

Compliments of
Security Trust and Savings Bank
Los Angeles, California

FIGURE 23. "Official Program: The Los Angeles Aqueduct and Exposition Park Celebration, November Fifth and Sixth, Nineteen Hundred and Thirteen."
Courtesy of the Seaver Center for Western History Research, Los Angeles County Museum of Natural History.

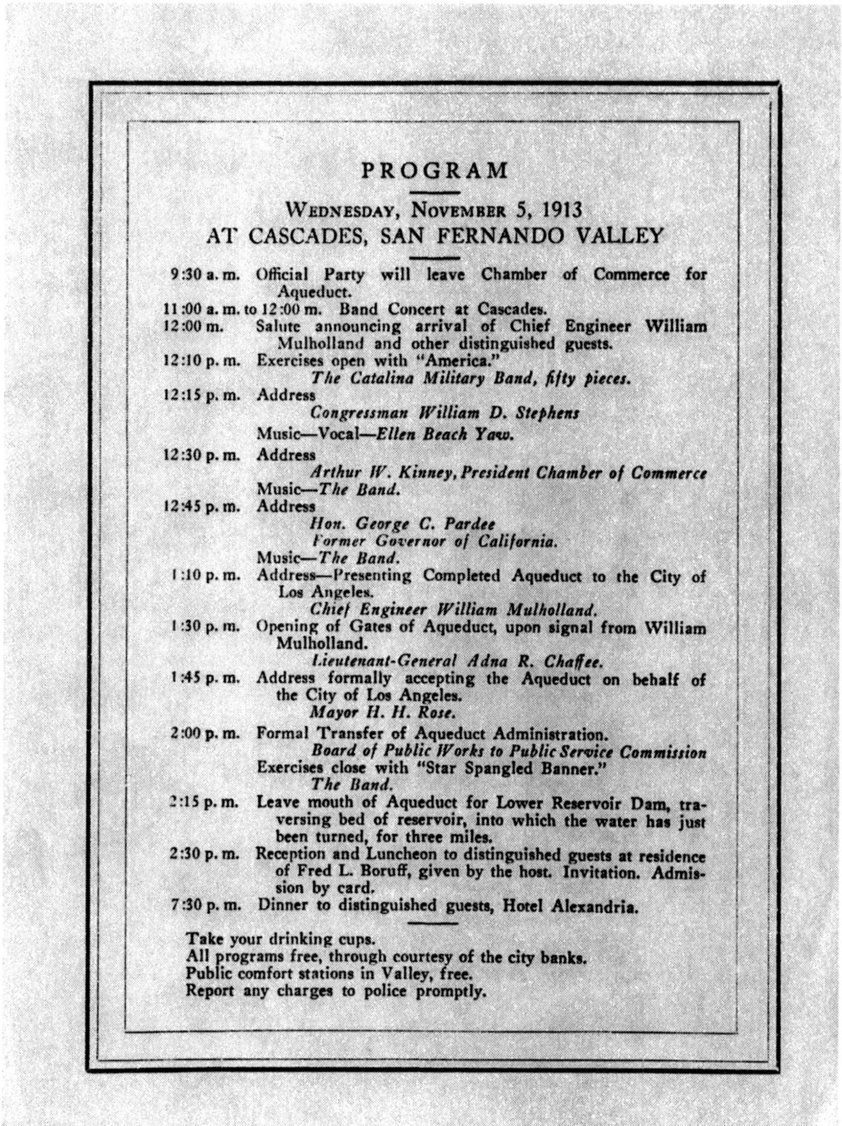

PROGRAM

WEDNESDAY, NOVEMBER 5, 1913
AT CASCADES, SAN FERNANDO VALLEY

9:30 a.m.   Official Party will leave Chamber of Commerce for Aqueduct.

11:00 a.m. to 12:00 m.   Band Concert at Cascades.

12:00 m.   Salute announcing arrival of Chief Engineer William Mulholland and other distinguished guests.

12:10 p.m.   Exercises open with "America."
The Catalina Military Band, fifty pieces.

12:15 p.m.   Address
Congressman William D. Stephens
Music—Vocal—*Ellen Beach Yaw.*

12:30 p.m.   Address
Arthur W. Kinney, President Chamber of Commerce
Music—*The Band.*

12:45 p.m.   Address
Hon. George C. Pardee
Former Governor of California.
Music—*The Band.*

1:10 p.m.   Address—Presenting Completed Aqueduct to the City of Los Angeles.
Chief Engineer William Mulholland.

1:30 p.m.   Opening of Gates of Aqueduct, upon signal from William Mulholland.
Lieutenant-General Adna R. Chaffee.

1:45 p.m.   Address formally accepting the Aqueduct on behalf of the City of Los Angeles.
Mayor H. H. Rose.

2:00 p.m.   Formal Transfer of Aqueduct Administration.
Board of Public Works to Public Service Commission
Exercises close with "Star Spangled Banner."
The Band.

2:15 p.m.   Leave mouth of Aqueduct for Lower Reservoir Dam, traversing bed of reservoir, into which the water has just been turned, for three miles.

2:30 p.m.   Reception and Luncheon to distinguished guests at residence of Fred L. Boruff, given by the host. Invitation. Admission by card.

7:30 p.m.   Dinner to distinguished guests, Hotel Alexandria.

Take your drinking cups.
All programs free, through courtesy of the city banks.
Public comfort stations in Valley, free.
Report any charges to police promptly.

FIGURE 24. "Official Program: The Los Angeles Aqueduct and Exposition Park Celebration, November Fifth and Sixth, Nineteen Hundred and Thirteen."

PROGRAM

Thursday, November 6, 1913
CITY AND EXPOSITION PARK

10:00 a. m. Industrial Parade in down-town Business District, leaving Temple and Spring Streets at 10 o'clock.

12:00 m. to 12:45 p. m. Band Concert, Sunken Garden, Exposition Park.

12:15 p. m. Official Party will leave Chamber of Commerce for Exposition Park.

12:30 to
2:30 p. m. Informal Reception—Music—State Exposition Building.

1:00 p. m. Exercises open with Music—*The Band.*

1:05 p. m. Address—"Exposition Park as a State Institution"—in front of State Exposition Building.

> *Senator Lee C. Gates, representing*
> *Governor Johnson.*

Music—*The Band.*

1:20 p. m. Dedication of Aqueduct Memorial Fountain Site, Sunken Garden.

Address

> *U. S. Senator John D. Works.*

1:35 p. m. Laying Cornerstone of the State (Seventh Regt.) Armory.

> *Auspices of Grand Lodge of California, F. & A. M.*

Music—*The Band.*

2:00 p. m. Address — Officially Opening the Los Angeles County Museum of History, Science and Art.

> *Hon. John D. Fredericks.*

2:30 p. m. Athletic Games on Exposition Park Infield Playground. No admission fees.

8:00 to
11:00 p. m. Reception to distinguished guests at Museum of History, Science and Art, by Board of Governors. Invitation.

Take your drinking cups.
Grand Stand seats free.
Public Comfort Stations in State and County buildings and on grounds free.
Sandwiches, 10c. Coffee, 10c.
Soft Drinks, 10c. Ice Cream, 10c. Pennants, 25c.
Pennants sold on streets, at Aqueduct, and in Exposition Park.
Report all violations to police promptly.

FIGURE 25. "Official Program: The Los Angeles Aqueduct and Exposition Park Celebration, November Fifth and Sixth, Nineteen Hundred and Thirteen."
Courtesy of the Seaver Center for Western History Research, Los Angeles County Museum of Natural History.

FIGURE 26. Investigators examining dynamite found near the aqueduct after several bombings. From the Los Angeles Times Photographic Archive, courtesy of Library Special Collections, Charles E. Young Research Library, UCLA.

This is only one chapter—but the most tragic—in a long story of tragedies in which the people of the Owens Valley have been the helpless victims of the Los Angeles City Water Board. . . .

In all history there was never a more flagrant example of one part of the country, politically and financially powerful, destroying a weaker section, and doing it without regard to obligations, moral or financial. There is more to the calamity in Inyo than appears on the surface, much more than simply a bank failure or sudden economic distress of a community. There is a story of injustices stretching over a period of years; of ruthless methods on the part of one group to crush another, smaller and more helpless; the story of an oppressed people and of stricken leaders. . . .

I do not minimize my brothers' mistakes. Neither is it possible for me to exaggerate the ruthlessness of the City Water Board of Los Angeles or the long, heart-breaking struggle between the City and Owens Valley, during which I know it was my brothers' highest aim to protect the people of the Valley who, with them have suffered for many years through the policy of the Water Board.

For whatever of wrong there was in my brothers' methods they are paying the supreme price. They are branded as criminals, while there is at large today, representing the City of Los Angeles, a group of men who, in my opinion, are *criminals* at *heart*. Men who deliberately planned the devastation of the Owens River country; who worked calculating, relentlessly, over a period of years for the destruction of our communities; who laid waste to our fields, uprooted and burned our orchards; who, through most malicious propaganda, shattered the confidence of the people, undermined our financial institutions and finally, at the crucial moment, cut off our credit on the outside, thereby precipitating the more recent calamity—the failure of the Banks. Do you not call *that* Crime? . . .

Today some of the same men are busy explaining the failure of the St. Francis Dam—a task that will undoubtedly occupy them for some time unless this crime also is successfully "white-washed;" while others of the group have for several months past been actively engaged in Washington trying to outwit, out-maneuver six other states for the monopoly of the Colorado River. And for what purpose? For the benefit of California as a State? Scarcely. For a city's domestic needs? Obviously not. For flood protection in the Imperial Valley? How ironical! That these men should show concern for the Imperial Valley, knowing well that no menace of Nature could be more disastrous to that Valley than their own political intrigue has been to Owens Valley.

Daily it is becoming more apparent to the public at large what has been to us for many years a flagrant fact, that politicians and not engineers were the builders of the Los Angeles Aqueduct. . . . A system consisting of a 200-mile aqueduct the safety of which depends on armed guards and machine guns; and numerous reservoirs and dams which only a miracle of the Almighty could make safe. . . .

If the Los Angeles Aqueduct whose waters spring so crystal clear from the snows of the Sierras, could reflect the tragedy of Owens Valley, that stream would run red from its very beginnings—red as the heart's blood of a valiant people!

· · ·

Other critics were helpful in devising a political strategy for the Watterson brothers to fight the Big City at the expense of farmers who would lose their bank savings. One of these critics offered to help—for a price.

From Burton Knisely to W. W. Watterson (November 18, 1926, as quoted in the *Municipal League of Los Angeles Bulletin* 5 [October 31, 1927]: 2).

I had envisioned myself helping outline and prepare the case and dividing its various phases among the witnesses and coaching them in their roles and seeing that we got the maximum obtainable publicity. * * * I will admit that if the project were abundantly financed I would think my brains, in devising the program, financing it and preparing our case[,] would deserve a reasonable reward. * * * I don't know whom you would wish to choose as your witnesses but for instance if in addition to yourself and myself we had Mr. Yandell with his long and intimate knowledge and his manner and capacity on the stand, Harry Glasscock with the atmosphere of tragedy he could work up, some good man on the City reparations angle, perhaps another ruined rancher of advanced age and two ruined women or perhaps just the first three men indicated and three women—couldn't we take up the Committee's time for three weeks and cause some commotion. I'm confident we could make the entire nation sit up and take notice. * * * With this as a beginning, we might raise more money. We ought to be able to supplement the sum from other sources. The City of Los Angeles is out in front as the flag-bearer and the champion and the pure white example of municipal ownership for the entire nation. * * * THE SHOWING UP OF LOS ANGELES IN HER TRUE COLORS IS WORTH MILLIONS TO THE PRIVATELY OWNED PUBLIC UTILITIES OF THE COUNTRY TO SAY NOTHING OF A MERE $3000 AND IF WE CAN REACH THE RIGHT SOURCES WE OUGHT TO BE ABLE TO ADD TO THE RESOURCES FOR OUR SHOW.

· · ·

The *Los Angeles Times* proved to be a stalwart and reliable defender of the aqueduct and of the city's purchase of further land and water rights in Owens Valley. Harrison Gray Otis, one of the paper's founders and father-in-law of the *Times* publisher in this era, had been one of the members of the land syndicate that profited from escalating land values in the San Fernando Valley when Owens River water became available there after 1915. The following *Times* editorial argues for more taxpayer-funded bonds for the project seventeen years after its completion.

From "Why $38,800,000?" *Los Angeles Times* (May 16, 1930).

The item of $6,660,000 for the purchase of all water and land rights of ranchers in Owens Valley and Long Valley represents a schedule of values in line with prices heretofore paid by the city of Los Angeles for similar resources. Moreover, acquisition of such rights will give Los Angeles undisputed ownership to all ranch water rights in Owens Valley and remove the menace of water litigation designed to sharply curtail the present utilization of water by this community. . . .

EVERY POSSIBLE SAFEGUARD HAS BEEN EMPLOYED TO PREVENT INFLATION OF VALUES AND TO FRUSTRATE ANY EFFORT AT PROFIT-TAKING BY OWNERS' REPRESEN-TATIVES, OPTIONERS, AGENTS, POLITICIANS OR ANY INDIVIDUAL OF GROUP OF INDI-VIDUALS OTHER THAN THE BONA FIDE OWNERS THEMSELVES. THE TIMES HAS GIVEN PARTICULAR ATTENTION TO THIS PHASE OF THE SITUATION AND IS CONVINCED THAT ADEQUATE PRECAUTION HAS BEEN PROVIDED TO PROTECT LOS ANGELES TAXPAYERS FROM THE SCHEMES OF THOSE WHO ORDINARILY SEEK TO EXPLOIT NEEDED PUBLIC IMPROVEMENTS FOR THE PURPOSE OF SELFISH PRIVATE GAIN. SO FAR AS SUCH MAT-TERS CAN BE DETERMINED BY FAIR AND EXPERT MEANS, THE TIMES BELIEVES THE PRICES AGREED UPON ARE JUSTIFIED. IF THE PRESSING NEED OF THE CITY FOR THE FACILITIES TO BE PROVIDED IS PROPERLY WEIGHED IT WILL APPEAR THAT THE LAND AND WATER VALUATIONS ARE EXCEEDINGLY ADVANTAGEOUS TO LOS ANGELES.

· · ·

Humorist Will Rogers gets the final word on the Owens River project here, although the controversy surrounding this chapter of Los Angeles and California history continues today.

From Will Rogers (in Bishop, California) to the editor, *Los Angeles Times* (August 25, 1932; letter of Will Rogers used with permission from Will Rogers Productions).

> Ten years ago this was a wonderful valley with one-quarter of a million acres of fruit and alfalfa. But Los Angeles had to have more water for the Chamber of Commerce to drink more toasts to growth, more water to dilute its orange juice, to water its geraniums for the tourists, while the giant cottonwoods here died. So now this is a valley of desolation, but wherever you find privation and oppressed people you find Democrats always bucking the giant octopus. Last night the local Democrats held a rally. Everybody in town, including the lone Republican (who, of course, is postmaster,) attended. He agreed to change his politics in return for his present office, it was unanimously passed, all adjourned. The politics is settled here for the next four years.
>
> Yours,
> Will Rogers

. . .

THE COLORADO RIVER

By the end of World War I, Los Angeles engineers were already searching for an additional water source as the city's population continued to grow. They joined with the U.S. Reclamation Service to build a high dam (Boulder Dam, or Boulder Canyon Dam, renamed Hoover Dam) on the Colorado River to store water and provide for flood control, the generation of electrical power, and several other purposes. The effort resulted in the 1922 agreement between the federal government and the seven states bordering the Colorado River to share the water for agricultural, residential, and industrial use and to compete for the hydroelectric power produced at the dam. Boosters in all of these states were interested in protecting their natural resources for use in future growth. Soon Los Angeles emerged as the leading force in the West to bring the project to fruition and obtain much of the water and resulting hydroelectricity for itself.

From the Colorado River Compact of the Seven States (1922, Huntington Library, San Marino, CA).

THE COLORADO RIVER COMPACT

The States of Arizona, California, Colorado Nevada, New Mexico, Utah, and Wyoming, having resolved to enter into a compact under the Act of the Congress of the United States of America approved August 19, 1921 (42 Statutes at Large, page 171), and the Acts of the legislatures of the said States, have through their Governors appointed as their Commissioners:

> W. S. Norviel for the State of Arizona
> W. F. McClure for the State of California

FIGURE 27. Hoover Dam (formerly Boulder Dam) in 1960.
Courtesy of the Los Angeles Public Library Photo Collection.

Ralph E. Carpenter for the State of Colorado
J. G. Scrugham for the State of Nevada
Stephen B. Davis, Jr., for the State of New Mexico
R. E. Caldwell for the State of Utah
Frank C. Emerson for the State of Wyoming

who, after negotiations participated in by Herbert Hoover appointed by The President as the representative of the United States of America, have agreed upon the following articles:

ARTICLE I

The major purposes of this compact are to provide for the equitable division and apportionment of the use of the waters of the Colorado River System; to establish the relative importance of different beneficial uses of water; to promote interstate comity; to remove causes of present and future controversies; and to secure the expeditious agricultural and industrial development of the Colorado River Basin, the storage of its waters, and the protection of life and property from floods. To these ends the Colorado River Basin is divided into two Basins, and an apportionment of the use of part of the water of the Colorado River System is made to each of them with the provision that further equitable apportionments may be made.

ARTICLE II

As used in this compact—

a. The term "Colorado River System" means that portion of the Colorado River and its tributaries within the United States of America.
b. The term "Colorado River Basin" means all of the drainage area of the Colorado River System and all other territory within the United States of America to which the waters of the Colorado River System shall be beneficially applied.
c. The term "States of the Upper Division" means the States of Colorado, New Mexico, Utah, and Wyoming.
d. The term "States of the Lower Division" means the States of Arizona, California, and Nevada.
e. The term "Lee Ferry" means a point in the main stream of the Colorado River one mile below the mouth of the Paria River.
f. The term "Upper Basin" means those parts of the States of Arizona, Colorado, New Mexico, Utah, and Wyoming within and from which waters naturally drain into the Colorado River System above Lee Ferry, and also all parts of said States located without the drainage area of the Colorado River System which are now or shall hereafter be beneficially served by waters diverted from the System above Lee Ferry.
g. The term "Lower Basin" means those parts of the States of Arizona, California, Nevada, New Mexico, and Utah within and from which waters naturally drain into the Colorado River System below Lee Ferry, and also all parts of said States located without the drainage area of the Colorado River System which are now or shall hereafter be beneficially served by waters diverted from the System below Lee Ferry.
h. The term "domestic use" shall include the use of water for household, stock, municipal, mining, industrial, and other like purposes, but shall exclude the generation of electrical power.

ARTICLE III

a. There is hereby apportioned from the Colorado River System in perpetuity to the Upper Basin and to the Lower Basin, respectively, the exclusive beneficial consumptive use of 7,500,000 acre-feet of water per annum, which shall include all water necessary for the supply of any rights which may now exist.
b. In addition to the apportionment in paragraph (a), the Lower Basin is hereby given the right to increase its beneficial consumptive use of such waters by one million acre-feet per annum.
c. If, as a matter of international comity, the United States of American shall hereafter recognize in the United States of Mexico any right to the use of any waters of the Colorado River System, such waters shall be supplied first from the waters which are surplus over and above the aggregate of the quantities specified

in paragraphs (a) and (b); and if such surplus shall prove insufficient for this purpose, then, the burden of such deficiency shall be equally borne by the Upper Basin and the Lower Basin, and whenever necessary the States of the Upper Division shall deliver at Lee Ferry water to supply one-half of the deficiency so recognized in addition to that provided in paragraph (d).

d. The States of the Upper Division will not cause the flow of the river at Lee Ferry to be depleted below an aggregate of 75,000,000 acre feet for any period of ten consecutive years reckoned in continuing progressive series beginning with the first day of October next succeeding the ratification of this compact.

e. The states of the Upper Division shall not withhold water, and the States of the Lower Division shall not require the delivery of water, which cannot reasonably be applied to domestic and agricultural uses.

f. Further equitable apportionment of the beneficial uses of the waters of the Colorado River System unapportioned by paragraphs (a), (b), and (c) may be made in the manner provided in paragraph (g) at any time after October first, 1963, if and when either Basin shall have reached its total beneficial consumptive use as set out in paragraphs (a) and (b).

g. In the event of a desire for further apportionment as provided in paragraph (f) any two signatory States, acting through their governors, may give joint notice of such desire to the Governors of the other signatory States and to The President of the United States of America, and it shall be the duty of the Governors of the signatory States and of The President of the United States of America forthwith to appoint representatives, whose duty it shall be to divide and apportion equitably between the Upper Basin and Lower Basin the beneficial use of the unapportioned water of the Colorado River System as mentioned in paragraph (f), subject to the legislative ratification of the signatory States and the Congress of the United States of America.

ARTICLE IV

a. Inasmuch as the Colorado River has ceased to be navigable for commerce and the reservation of its waters for navigation would seriously limit the development of its Basin, the use of its waters for purposes of navigation shall be subservient to the uses of such waters for domestic, agricultural, and power purposes. If the Congress shall not consent to this paragraph, the other provisions of this compact shall nevertheless remain binding.

b. Subject to the provisions of this compact, water of the Colorado River System may be impounded and used for the generation of electrical power, but such impounding and use shall be subservient to the use and consumption of such water for agricultural and domestic purposes and shall not interfere with or prevent use for such dominant purposes.

c. The provisions of this article shall not apply to or interfere with the regulation and control by any State within its boundaries of the appropriation, use, and distribution of water.

ARTICLE V

The chief official of each signatory State charged with the administration of water rights, together with the Director of the United States Reclamation Service and the Director of the United States Geological Survey shall cooperate, ex-officio:

a. To promote the systemic determination and coordination of the facts as to flow, appropriation, consumption, and use of water in the Colorado River Basin, and the interchange of available information in such matters.
b. To secure the ascertainment and publication of the annual flow of the Colorado River at Lee Ferry.
c. To perform such other duties as may be assigned by mutual consent of the signatories from time to time.

ARTICLE VI

Should any claim or controversy arise between any two or more of the signatory States: (a) with respect to the waters of the Colorado River System not covered by the terms of this compact; (b) over the meaning or performance of any of the terms of this compact; (c) as to the allocation of the burdens incident to the performance of any article of this compact or the delivery of waters as herein provided; (d) as to the construction or operation of works within the Colorado River Basin to be situated in two or more States, or to be constructed by one State for the benefit of another State; or (e) as to the diversion of water in one State for the benefit of another State; the Governors of the States affected, upon the request of one of them, shall forthwith appoint Commissioners with power to consider and adjust such claim or controversy, subject to ratification by the Legislatures of the States so affected.

Nothing herein contained shall prevent the adjustment of any such claim or controversy by any present method or by direct future legislative action of the interested States.

ARTICLE VII

Nothing in this compact shall be construed as affecting the obligations of the United States of America to Indian tribes.

ARTICLE VIII

Present perfected rights to the beneficial use of waters of the Colorado River System are unimpaired by this compact. Whenever storage capacity of 5,000,000 acre-feet shall have been provided to the main Colorado River within or for the benefit of the Lower Basin, then claims of such rights, if any, by appropriators or users of water in the Lower Basin against appropriators or users of water of the Upper Basin shall attach to and be satisfied from water that may be stored not in conflict with Article III.

All other rights to beneficial use of waters of the Colorado River System shall be satisfied solely from the water apportioned to that Basin in which they are situate.

ARTICLE IX

Nothing in this compact shall be construed to limit or prevent any State from instituting or maintaining any action or proceeding, legal or equitable, for the protection of any right under this compact or the enforcement of any of its provisions.

ARTICLE X

This compact may be terminated at any time by the unanimous agreement of the signatory States. In the event of such termination all rights established under it shall continue unimpaired.

ARTICLE XI

This compact shall become binding and obligatory when it shall have been approved by the Legislatures of each of the signatory States and by the Congress of the United States. Notice of approval by the Legislatures shall be given by the Governor of each signatory State to the Governors of the other signatory States and to the President of the United States, and the President of the United States is requested to give notice to the Governors of the signatory States of approval by the Congress of the United States.

IN WITNESS WHEREOF, the Commissioners have signed this compact in a single original, which shall be deposited in the archives of the Department of State of the United States of America and of which a duly certified copy shall be forwarded to the Governor of each of the signatory States.

DONE at the City of Santa Fe, New Mexico, this twenty-fourth day of November, A.D. One Thousand Nine Hundred and Twenty-two,

(Signed) W. S. Norviel
(Signed) W. F. McClure
(Signed) Delph E. Carpenter
(Signed) J. G. Scrugham
(Signed) Stephen B. Davis, Jr.
(Signed) R. E. Caldwell
(Signed) Frank C. Emerson

Approved:
(Signed) Herbert Hoover.

. . .

Negative views of the Colorado River project emerged from different sources. In one published response to a description of the undertaking, novelist Mary Austin, who had lived in the Owens Valley, likened it to the Los Angeles Aqueduct in Owens Valley.[1] The latter project was currently contested by many Owens Valley residents as Los Angeles continued to drain the valley of water while awaiting the additional water the city would draw from the Colorado River only two decades later. They saw the grasping hand of the Big City again grabbing resources and profits at the expense of farmers and everyone else.

Business leaders in Los Angeles were wary of some aspects of the project, but were wholeheartedly behind the effort to acquire more water for residential and industrial growth in the region. The Los Angeles Chamber of Commerce was one of many that lobbied Congress to approve the project. *Sunset* magazine, a longtime media outlet for corporations and boosters in the West, could be relied on to place the project in the best light as a crucial and urgent necessity for regional growth and prosperity.

From Lucius K. Chase (vice chairman, Citizens' Committee of Fifteen), "The C. of C. Plan for Colorado River" (*Southern California Business* 4 [November 1925]: 13, 40–41).

CHAMBER'S STAND

The stand of the Chamber set forth in a document signed by President R. W. Pridham was presented to the Senate Committee on Irrigation and Reclamation at its recent hearings held in Los Angeles.

The statement presented follows:

"The Los Angeles Chamber of Commerce, in connection with the investigation now being made by the United States Senate Committee on Irrigation and Reclamation now in session in this city, makes the following recommendations:

"1. We favor the construction of a high dam at or near Boulder Canyon in the Colorado river, for the following reasons: Such a dam will prevent flood destruction and give flood protection to the lands in the Parker Indian Reservation and the Yuma project in Arizona, and the Imperial and Palo Verde Valleys in California; will create a great reservoir of water to serve Los Angeles and other communities of the Southwest whose rapid growth will soon vitally need this as a dependable source of supply; will make available a large volume of hydro-electric energy, an important necessity for agricultural, industrial and community development in the Southwest; will permit the states of the lower basin with safety to approve the proposed compact between the seven states interested in the waters of the river; and for the further reason that it is a great economic waste to allow the flood waters of the river to spend themselves in the Gulf of California when by impounding them they can be made productive of great wealth and added prosperity to our nation.

"2. We also favor due and proper protection of the rights of all the other states having an interest in the waters of the Colorado river basin, and believe that all their rights should be justly and equitably considered and protected.

URGE ACTION

"3. We recommend that the Congress of the United States at its coming session should enact legislation providing for the construction of such a dam.

"4. That the waters conserved by the erection of said high dam be used exclusively for the irrigation and reclamation of lands within the United States and that proper provision be made in order that the United States soldiers and sailors may obtain the benefit of such reclaimed lands.

"5. That the United States lend its assistance so far as practicable and when found feasible to the building of the necessary canals and distributing works in order that the water so conserved may be distributed to the lands within the United States, which will now or may hereafter be irrigated by such waters and that such canals and distributing works be located exclusively within the territory of the United States, if the same is found possible or practicable.

"6. That the right to generate and distribute the hydro-electric energy which may be developed by the said dam be sold to municipalities and other agencies which may have the facilities for the development and distribution of the same at such a price as will repay the United States government within a reasonable time the entire cost of the said dam in excess of such sums as the United States government may deem fit to contribute toward such flood control, which we estimate should be about thirty million dollars."

From "Southern California Needs Colorado River Water" (*Sunset* 56 [March 1926]: 50, 98; permission courtesy of the Sunset Publishing Corporation).

When there is not a sufficient supply of water to support both agriculture and human beings in a given area the former must do without water. That is a law of life, and the thickly populated section of Southern California is developing a condition which will test that law unless protective means are adopted.

The conflict of urban interests and country interests is already a fact down there. So those who understand the situation are in deadly earnest in their efforts to hasten settlement of the Colorado river controversy so some of the millions of gallons of its water, now wasted, can be used to permit the natural development of that section.

The coastal plain extending from the Pacific ocean to the base of the Puente hills and Santa Monica mountains and from the mountains to the San Joaquin hills, covering an area of 775 square miles, was originally saturated with ground water, held back by the coastal barriers. Most of that water has been used.

Orange county employed J. B. Lippincott, a Los Angeles engineer, to make a survey of the situation, and his report on water conservation and flood control of the Santa Ana river revealed astounding facts. His investigations proved that during the ten years preceding July 1, 1925, the amount of water pumped from the underground basin of Orange county had increased 300 percent!

In 1888 the total artesian area in the entire coastal plain was 315 square miles. In 1904 it had been reduced to 206 square miles. At the beginning of 1925 it had nearly disappeared, the total area being only 55 square miles.

One test well was put down in Southern California in the late nineties and it has been watched carefully in the study of the underground water supply. At the start there was sufficient pressure to raise the water 60 feet above the ground surface. In the summer of 1924 the water level had dropped 50 feet below the surface, a total decline of 110 feet since the well was first observed!

With the population in the cities gaining rapidly and steadily, and with demand for water for domestic purposes growing in proportion, it is inevitable that horticultural and agricultural interests will suffer unless the total water supply can be increased.

"We need the Colorado river water," declared J. P. Baumgartner, publisher of the Santa Ana *Register,* to the writer of The Pulse department of *Sunset Magazine.* "Unless a new supply of water is brought in, you will see orange groves chopped down. The fight between the farmers and the cities of Southern California for water is already in progress."

It is generally taken for granted by those without specific knowledge that the Owens river and the famous aqueduct built by the city of Los Angeles are capable of supplying all future needs. There is also a common belief that Los Angeles is using its source of water as a club with which to force neighboring cities to ask for annexation.

"Neighboring cities have been knocking at the doors of Los Angeles for water," declared W. W. Hurlbut, office engineer for the Los Angeles Bureau of Water Works and Supply. "But the growth of Los Angeles has been so rapid that it can not spare water for the future. This department, consequently, sent a resolution to the city council suggesting that any city joining Los Angeles to be required to take care of its own water needs until a supplementary source is developed. By the time the Colorado river can be dammed and an aqueduct can be built to Los Angeles, this city will be ready for the additional water."

For the fiscal year ending June 30, 1925, the water department installed 20,000 new services, and the 1920 Federal census proved that there were 5.4 inhabitants per service!

The water department now gives service all the way up from sea level to 1450 feet above sea level.

If a dam is built in the Boulder or Black cañon of the Colorado river, water for Los Angeles will be taken out sixty-five miles below Needles, Cal., and raised 1700 feet to the aqueduct! Power for the pumps will be generated by water falling over the dam.

The aqueduct will be 258 miles in length, 20 miles longer than the present one from Owens river. It will be three and three-fourths times as large as the Owens river aqueduct. But though cost of material and the wage scale have greatly advanced since the latter was built and though the cost of the new aqueduct has been estimated at approximately $150,000,000, the per capita cost will not exceed that of the Owens river project, so rapid has been the population increase.

Under the Colorado river plan, Los Angeles would receive 1000 second-feet of water and neighboring cities and towns would receive 500 second-feet. This would give Los Angeles an increase of 969,472,000 gallons a day as compared with 258,000,000 gallons a day now available, and with a per capita consumption of 148 gallons a day during the hot months of 1925 and with an average daily per capita consumption of 123 gallons during the fiscal year ending June 30, 1925.

Students of city development, with national reputations, freely predict that within twenty-five years the metropolitan area of Los Angeles will contain several millions of inhabitants. So when the magnitude of the Colorado river proposal is considered and the time required for completion is taken into account, the seriousness of delay is obvious.

· · ·

The main element that prompted opposition to the project—other than what some critics perceived as utter domination by Los Angeles because of its insatiable desire for water and hydroelectric power—was the stipulation that hydroelectric power produced at the Boulder Canyon Dam would be sold to both municipalities and private power companies to recoup the construction and operation costs of the federal government. In Los Angeles, as well as across the nation, allowing cities to buy power for municipal systems became a political issue for private-enterprise adherents, who did not mind local governments distributing water. In this passage from a then-contemporary pamphlet, a representative of a private utility organization criticized this element of the plan.

From Frank Bohn, ed., *The Boulder Canyon Dam: The Essence of the Swing-Johnson Bill* ([n.p.: National Utilities Association, 1927], 3–6, held by Special Collections, Claremont Colleges Library, Claremont, CA, http://ccdl.libraries.claremont.edu/ cdm/).

ELEVEN POINTS

The following pages contain the facts as to the proposals urged in Congress for the development of the Colorado River at National expense. There are many angles, and the documents are voluminous, but the principles involved may be summarized in a few paragraphs.

1. There is danger of property loss in the Imperial Valley in California from the Colorado River floods. Flood protection is essential to the well-being of the people of that valley.
2. Boulder Dam is not primarily for flood control. It has three great purposes for which it is alleged a high dam is essential: First, storage of water for irrigation in the Imperial Valley; second, the furnishing of a domestic water supply for the city of Los Angeles, and third, the development of electric power.
3. Flood control on the Mississippi has been carefully worked out. It has been studied for years. The Army Engineers will present to Congress at its next session a comprehensive plan based upon detailed investigation. The situation on the Colorado is exactly the opposite. There is no study, no report, no complete plan. No one knows what the right way is. We have merely the suggestion that Boulder Dam would serve the purpose.
4. The reason for this anomalous situation lies in the fact that, when the appropriation was passed authorizing the Army Engineers to determine methods of flood control on the Mississippi and other rivers of the United States, the advocates of the Los Angeles project were able to write in a provision that no part of the funds could be used for investigation of flood control on the Colorado River. They themselves prevented Congress from obtaining the information on which to act intelligently.
5. There have been a few reports on the engineering features of Boulder Dam, as distinct from the river as a whole, notably a voluminous one of eight volumes

by the Reclamation Service, but nothing directed specifically to the ascertainment of the best method of flood control.

6. Obviously, the first step in providing flood control on the Colorado should be the ascertainment of the facts and the determination of proper methods.

7. It has been frequently asserted that flood danger can be eliminated from the Colorado at a cost of $10,000,000 or less, in contrast with the $125,000,000 estimated under the Los Angeles plan. Investigation will demonstrate whether the statements are true.

8. Disregarding flood control, the other purposes of the project represent merely local improvements for Southern California to be made at National expense. The bill is properly called "The Los Angeles Water and Power Bill." There seems no reason why the taxpayers of Virginia, or Kansas, or any other state, should furnish municipal water for that city. If it be said that the funds are merely advanced, and that it is expected that the sale of electric power will reimburse the Federal government, the answer is that the United States has never heretofore entered into the business of financing municipalities, and that if it is now to undertake that new activity, there will be no end. Los Angeles is not the only ambitious city in the country, nor the only one willing that the Nation would assume its financial burdens.

9. Boulder Dam is to be constructed with an above surface height of about 600 feet. Its foundation will be 127 feet lower down, at bed rock. The total height will therefore be about 700 feet, twice as high as any dam in the world. The dam would contain nearly four million yards of concrete, three times as much as the Assuan Dam in Egypt. No such mass of masonry has ever been thrown together in engineering history. Excavations for the foundations will amount to more than a million cubic yards of material, equivalent to the space occupied by two city blocks solid with ten-story buildings, and must be done between flood stages of the river. Wholly novel engineering problems must be solved. Yet it is proposed to enter upon this stupendous undertaking merely upon the advice of the Reclamation Service of the United States, seriously questioned by many engineers, and which presents what the Secretary of the Interior has himself declared to be an insufficient basis. Here again thorough study is indicated before action.

10. The present proposal authorizes the Secretary of the Interior, in his discretion, to build and operate a power plant in connection with the dam, and to sell the current produced. It would thus put the Government directly into the business of generating and selling electric power. It is directly contrary to the principle controlling in National affairs, that the government should confine itself to governing and not enter the field of business, which belongs to the individual. The proponents of the measure openly state that this is merely the opening gun in the campaign for government ownership and operation of public utilities. Apparently, they are threatened with the same baptism of fire which the railroads suffered and from which they finally emerged alive but badly burned. Nothing could be worse for the American people than to paralyze their present efficient service by the dead hand of government.

11. The attitude of the public should be complete support for any sane plan for flood control, absolute opposition to any scheme for putting the government into private business.

. . .

Many arguments in favor of the Colorado River project celebrated it as a public development of a natural resource that would bring about national benefit to millions. One such plea for public development of water and hydroelectric power was made by Gifford Pinchot, former chief of the U.S. Forest Service and a leader in the national Progressive Party in the early twentieth century.

From Gifford Pinchot, "Who Owns Our Rivers" (*The Nation* 126 [January 18, 1928]: 64–66 [©2016 The Nation Company, LLC. All rights reserved. Used by permission and protected by the Copyright Laws of the United States. The printing, copying, redistribution, or retransmission of this Content without express written permission is prohibited]).

"WHO OWNS OUR RIVERS?"

The Boulder Dam project supplies one of the most important problems before the present Congress. I would like to lead you to it along a winding trail. Three-fourths of the earth's surface is water. But when you step off an ocean liner and come ashore you do not leave the water question behind you. The problem changes from salt water to fresh, but it does not evaporate. Of all the natural resources water on land is in one sense the most fundamental and the most clamorous for attention, just as the forest is in another sense.

A great part of man's task on the land is dealing with water, because next to the air we breathe water is the most essential thing in human life. The number of people who can live in the United States is determined not by the available amount of land but by the available amount of water. We have land enough for a far larger population than will ever inhabit the United States for the simple reason that we lack water enough to make all the land fertile and productive. Millions of arid and semiarid acres lie out under the sun to prove it. It takes many tons of water to grow an acre of corn. It takes additional tons of water to transform that corn into hogs. Forty acres without water will produce neither a single ear of corn nor a single pork chop.

Water, then, is indispensable, but as with other good things it is easily possible to have too much of it. We are apt to speak of fire as the destroying element, but an excess of water is far more destructive than an excess of fire. The greatest natural calamity in the history of the United States, the recent Mississippi flood, was due to too much water at one time in the wrong place.

The chief conservation problem facing the people of the United States is the control of our river systems. There are three river problems which have become immediate issues before Congress. One is that of the Mississippi, brought to a head by the great flood of a year ago; another, that of Muscle Shoals on the Tennessee; the third, that of Boulder Canyon. In all three the development of electric power has become a crucial question, and for precisely the same reason. Briefly the issue is, For whose benefit shall the power be developed?

I would not have you understand that the question of electric power is the only one involved in Boulder Canyon. Navigation to some extent, irrigation to a very large extent, and flood control are all intimately involved; and so is the domestic and industrial water-supply for more than a million people in and around Los Angeles.

The Colorado River is formed by the junction of the Green and the Grand rivers in the State of Utah. From its headwaters to the Gulf it flows through or past seven States. There are along it thirteen principal power sites capable of developing three or four million water horsepower. Along its course in Arizona and California, and Mexico as well, are millions of acres of irrigable lands now desert; and near its mouth is the Imperial Valley, partly in California and partly in Mexico, inhabited mainly by American citizens, and redeemed from utter barrenness by water from the Colorado River.

Most of Imperial Valley, moreover, is below sea level, and there is serious danger that the Colorado, which flows past it at a high elevation, will break into this deep hole as it did into the Salton Sink and change a land of fertile farms into a Dead Sea.

In order to prevent this calamity it is proposed to build at Boulder Canyon, a dam twice as high as the next highest dam in the world, and create a reservoir a hundred miles long, capable of holding the entire flow of the Colorado for more than a year. This dam will make flood control certain and secure. At the same time it will develop from 600,000 to 1,000,000 continuous horse-power. And that is what the trouble is all about.

If there were no power question involved the Boulder Dam Bill would meet nothing but smiles. The bill authorizes (but does not direct) the Secretary of the Interior to construct electric-power-generating works in connection with the dam, and sell the power for distribution to municipalities or to private power corporations. If the Government makes and sells that power, it can incorporate in the contract of sale such conditions as will insure ultimate justice to the consumer.

That is important to the domestic consumer especially (which means pretty nearly all of us) because the power companies have been making us pay several times as much as we ought to pay. It is important to the companies because they have been, and are now, charging us several times as much as they could afford to serve us for. Which brings us to the essential question: Shall the Government be authorized to build the power works at Boulder Dam, and so get a chance to protect the rest of us from the present extortion? Or shall the Government, having built the dam, let some private company build the works, and so lose the chance to prevent extortion? That is the gist of the whole matter.

There are, of course, complications. So vast a project could hardly be without them. Certain of the States through which the Colorado River flows demand that this great national project shall take second place to the States' Rights theory and the individual interests of the States. Arizona, for example, proposes to hold up the project unless she can be guaranteed what amounts to the right to tax national property used for the creation of electric power in the Colorado River. As a representative of Arizona said to me, "We propose to make the Government pay just as if it was a private company."

But the more serious danger comes from the electric-power companies, which are also suspected of being behind some of the obstructive demands of the States. The object of the power companies is to prevent the establishment of a government standard by which their own rates to consumers of electric power can be measured. Their objection to the construction of Boulder Dam has nothing to do with the dam itself but is wholly centered in the power-generating works through which the Government, under the Swing-Johnson Bill, is authorized to utilize the hydro-electric energy made available by the dam.

The Government does not propose to go into the business of selling power to the consumer. What it contemplates doing at Boulder Dam is what it is already doing at a number of government-built irrigation dams, namely, to transform into electric current the energy produced by the dam and to sell that current for distribution either by municipalities or private corporations. It does not propose to go into the power business but merely to produce the current, leaving to other agencies its distribution to the consumer.

That this is a proper function of the Government is attested not only by common sense but also by the man who has a better right to speak for the power industry than any other in America—Owen D. Young, head of the General Electric Company. In a speech on May 18, 1926, to the National Electric Light Association, Mr. Young said:

> There is a class of water-powers which, in my judgment, must be separately considered. No suggestion has yet been made which adequately meets their needs. Where vast rivers either on international boundaries or within the United States require development for several purposes, such as navigation, irrigation, and flood control as well as for power, there arises a new kind of question which is wholly unrelated to the old controversy of government versus private ownership. The discussion of this question has been clouded by the old animosities. The private-ownership people feel that if the Government has anything to do with the development of power in these composite situations, it will be merely the starting-point from which the advocates of public ownership will advance their operations. On the other hand, the public-ownership people feel that the privately owned companies which seek to throw dams in these great rivers, and incidentally perforce take over the effective navigation, irrigation, and flood control, are so intrenching themselves in purely public operations as not only to make all thought of public ownership impossible, but to create instruments of oppression rather than of service. While this debate goes on, vast rivers go unharnessed for power, waterways are undeveloped, floods drown us, and droughts devour us. May I not call for a broader view in the public interest from the representatives of both the utilities and the public? . . .

Much has been made of the question as to whether these dams should be built and owned by the Government. If the dams really serve the great purposes of navigation and flood control, which are clearly governmental activities, then it seems to me public ownership of them cannot be objected to. Personally, I prefer that the construction and ownership of such an enterprise be in the hands of a public corporation, the stock of which should be government-owned, with the provision that that corporation finance the enterprise with its own securities.

Mr. Young favors the public development of the Long Sault rapids on the St. Lawrence and the public construction of the power works there. Where he stands on the Swing-Johnson Bill I do not know, but the electric industry takes precisely the position which he does not take in the quotation above, and has today a great lobby in Washington to defeat the Boulder Dam project.

The power companies have four lines of defense against the establishment of a government standard at Boulder Canyon. The front-line trenches are built to prevent the passage of the bill altogether, thus destroying the Government's power not only to protect the consumer of electricity but also to protect the farmers of Imperial Valley against flood. This first line held at the last session of Congress. If the power companies can persuade Congress to defer action till the several States along the Colorado settle all their differences, and then can keep the States from agreeing, this first line may hold indefinitely.

The second line intends to restrict the Government's action solely to the construction of a flood-prevention dam, which need not be at Boulder Canyon and which would produce either a comparatively negligible amount of electricity or no electricity at all.

The third line is to prevent government-built electricity-generating works from being attached to the Boulder Dam project. The electric interests baldly offered at the last session to allow the passage of the Boulder Dam Bill provided the authority to construct these generating works was cut out.

But if they are defeated here and Boulder Dam is built with the government generating works attached, then the fourth line of defense of the power people is to saddle the government-made current with every possible or impossible expense, with the immediate hope of hampering the enterprise and the more distant hope of making the Government's undertaking fail altogether.

Here is where the demand of Arizona and Nevada for the right to tax government property fits the hand of the power companies like a glove. If Arizona can add its taxes to the cost of the power produced, if Nevada can do likewise, if later the similar claims of other States can add still further to the burden, then perhaps the power interests, driven out of their first, second, and third lines of defense, may still be able to hold out.

The vastness of the stake for which the power companies are playing must never be forgotten. Boulder Canyon is to them not a question of Los Angeles or California or Arizona or any of the seven States of the Colorado Basin. It is a question of the value to its owners of the gigantic electric monopoly now forming all over the United States—its value measured in excessive rates to the consumer. On no other theory can their nation-wide opposition to Boulder Canyon be explained or understood. And just there lies your interest and mine in what is about to happen at a spot in the Colorado River that very few of us have ever seen or ever will.

· · ·

Federal and Los Angeles officials were convinced of the need for the project, and they stressed the benefits that would accrue well beyond the city or metropolitan limits of Los Angeles. U.S. secretary of the interior and future U.S. president Herbert Hoover and the Los Angeles Water Bureau chief engineer William Mulholland proved especially effective boosters in this regard. In one planning journal, the two contributed essays addressing the importance of the project.

From Herbert Hoover, "The Colorado River Problem" (*The Community Builder: Regional Planning, Rural Planning, City and Town Planning Monthly* 1 [March 1928]: 9–12; held by Special Collections, Claremont Colleges Library, Claremont, CA).

The next most important line of conflict is over the character and location of the first works to be erected on the river. I believe the largest group of those who have dealt with the problem, both engineers and business folk, have come to the conclusion that there should be a high dam erected somewhere in the vicinity of Black Canyon. That is known usually as the Boulder Canyon site, but nevertheless it is actually Black Canyon. The dam so erected is proposed to serve the triple purpose of power, flood control, and storage. Perhaps I should state them in a different order—flood control, storage, and power, as power is a by product of these other works.

There are theoretical engineering reasons why flood control and storage works should be erected farther up the river and why storage works should be erected farther down the river; and I have not any doubt that given another century of development on the river all things will be done. The problem that we have to consider, however, what will serve the next generation in the most economical manner, and we must take capital expenditure and power markets into consideration in determining this. I can conceive the development of probably 15 different dams on the Colorado River, the securing of 6,000,000 or 7,000,000 horsepower; but the only place where there is an economic market for power today, at least of any consequence, is in Southern California, the economical distance for the most of such dams being too remote for that market. No doubt markets will grow in time so as to warrant the construction of dams all up and down the river. We have to consider here the problem of financing; that in the erection of a dam—or of any works for that matter—we must make such recovery as we can on the cost, and therefore we must find an immediate market for power. For that reason it seems to be that logic drives us as near to the power market as possible, and that it therefore takes us down into the lower canyon.

I do not believe that construction at that point is going to interfere with the systematic development of the Colorado River for storage and power above and below. As I have said, I think the time will come when a storage dam should probably be erected below Boulder Canyon and that storage dams and flood control dams will be erected far above. Those who have looked into the engineering problems involved will recognize that the operation of a single dam for the triple purpose is rather difficult and will not give the maximum power results. For instance, such a dam must be partly empty in anticipation of the spring flood and hence the power possibilities will be much diminished, and beyond this it will be necessary thereafter to lower the head for irrigation purposes. Thus the power production from such a dam will be rather irregular.

But in any event, I do not believe that we can not now contemplate the expenditure of the several hundred of millions of dollars necessary to carry out the theoretical plan; we should confine ourselves to what we can afford to spend now, and I do not believe we will destroy the possibilities of the river for systematic development by this course. We must await a settlement of population and their demands to create a need for the future development.

The proposed Black Canyon Dam of 540 feet, as estimated by the reclamation engineers, would cost about $41,000,000 or $42,000,000. The cost of an electrical generation plant to go with it would be about another $33,000,000. And the transmission lines to the power market would be somewhere about $27,000,000 more, or a total of from $110,000,000 to $115,000,000 for dam and equipment. The loss of interest during construction would be $10,000,000 more. The alternative plan of a 606-foot dam would require something like $20,000,000 more.

Now, the 540 foot dam would apparently develop, theoretically at least, about 550,000 primary horsepower and another 450,000 secondary horsepower. No engineer could say at the present moment what the actual power development will be, because none of us know until we have had experience how much the electrical power will need to be made subjective to flood control and irrigation in the manner I have referred to[,] but in any event these theoretic figures are possibly near enough.

Now a large part of the power developed will be needed to pump the water for the proposed domestic water supply plan for Southern California and both the manufacturers and private power companies will need the surplus power. It seems to me we need some consideration here of making a settled financial plan if we are to expedite this very urgently needed development. The people of Southern California have recognized that the folk in the Eastern and Central states will probably not be anxious for the Federal Government to fund the whole of the $115,000,000 for this development, and they have already expressed their willingness to make a substantial contribution to it, both from the municipalities and from the private power companies. It seems to me that the Federal Government has a very substantial obligation in this matter. It has been traditional to provide flood control in the protection of our people at the cost of the Federal Government, and we, of course, have the reclamation funds for the development of arid land; so that here is a problem of the proper contribution from municipalities, irrigation districts, private power companies, and the Federal Government.

All this leads me to the belief that somebody ought to be given authority to negotiate a definite financial contract which could be laid before Congress for approval in connection with the construction of these works. It does not seem to me it would take long to do that, and it could possibly be laid on the table here before this session of Congress expires. I believe that we should do all we can to expedite this matter. It is true that our path would have been smoother if we could have had more success in the ratification of the compact, but so long as we have these great conflicts and differences of view that I have mentioned we must expect difficulties. And in this connection I would remind you that it required, I believe, 10 or 11 years to secure a ratification of the Federal Constitution, and I doubt if there was as much emotion connected with that proposition as there is with water rights between seven States. So we may make progress more speedily than was made by the original thirteen States of this Union.

From William Mulholland, "Water from the Colorado" (*The Community Builder: Regional Planning, Rural Planning, City and Town Planning Monthly* 1 [March 1928]: 23, held by Special Collections, Claremont Colleges Library, Claremont, CA).

California, in common with many other states throughout the Far West, measures her advancement in agriculture, industry and population by the yardstick of water and hydro-electric power of development.

Twenty years ago, Los Angeles, with a constantly mounting population, began to reach the limit of its local water supply. Beyond the banks of the Los Angeles River, which had served the city faithfully from its establishment as a Spanish pueblo in 1787 [actually, 1781], there was no other obvious large water supply source within reach. Then we discovered the Owens River, 250 miles to the north, and fed by the melting snows of the High Sierras. There were those who regarded the construction of the Owens River Aqueduct as an impossible engineering undertaking, but the job was completed within the original cost estimate of $24,000,000, and Owens River water was brought to Los Angeles—enough to supply 2,000,000 people.

Los Angeles believed it had solved its water problem for two generations, at the least. Today, only thirteen years after the completion of the aqueduct, however, we find our city rapidly approaching its second million in population, and we are already completing plans for a second much greater water project.

There are no more streams, small or large, within the boundaries of the state which may be developed by the great cities of Southern California. Fortunately, however, California is bordered on the east by one of the greatest rivers in America, the Colorado.

Before the water of the Colorado can be put to use, either for power development or domestic use in Southern California, however, it is essential that its present dangerous and wasteful flow be regulated by the construction of a high flood control and storage dam.

· · ·

The Colorado River project became an opportunity for Southern California municipalities to acquire water for future development. A number of these cities,

FIGURE 28. Parker Dam is a much smaller structure than Boulder/Hoover Dam and is located farther south on the Colorado River. Built by the Metropolitan Water District in the 1930s, it began releasing water to Southern California in 1941 through the Colorado River Aqueduct. This image is from April 1, 1966.
From the Otis Marston Collection, P042/0006, courtesy of The Huntington Library, San Marino, California.

led by Los Angeles, created the Metropolitan Water District of Southern California as an agency to plan, build, and finance the system that would bring and distribute water from Parker Dam, located just below Boulder Dam, beginning in 1941. The legislation to create this district was debated in the 1925 session of the California Legislature at a time when municipal ownership advocates in Los Angeles and the conservative owner of the *Los Angeles Times* were in a heated political battle. So it is not surprising that *Times* reporter Kyle Palmer described the legislation as a resort to socialism on the part of the opposition. The bill finally passed in 1927, and in the following years Metropolitan Water District officials made many attempts to explain why it was needed for future growth in Los Angeles and the rest of Southern California.

From Kyle D. Palmer, "Water Act Up Today" (*Los Angeles Times*, April 1, 1925 [Kyle D. Palmer and Los Angeles Staff. Copyright © 1925. Los Angeles Times. Reprinted with Permission]).

"WATER ACT UP TODAY
DEFEAT OF BILL CERTAIN
LEGISLATURE EXPECTED TO HALT CRAFTY SCHEME OF LOCAL POWER BUREAU CLIQUE
MEASURE DESIGNED TO BUILD UP GIGANTIC POLITICAL MACHINE EXPOSED"

SACRAMENTO. March 31—Inspired and devised by the same clique of municipal ownership faddists that has sought to use the Los Angeles Water and Power Bureau as a superpolitical machine, the so-called metropolitan water district bill purporting to create opportunity for municipal cooperation in distribution of water from the Colorado River will be debated in Senate committee tomorrow.

The status of this measure, one of the most Socialistic proposals ever submitted to a California Legislature, is unique in the history of the State and its defeat is deemed certain.

The four nominal authors of the bill, Senator Johnson of Pasadena, Senator Swing of San Bernardino, Assemblyman Weller of Glendale and Assemblyman Jones of Ontario, who agreed in good faith to urge adoption of the proposal under the impression that it was a beneficial act, are themselves unaware of all its ramifications despite the introduction of eighty-six amendments.

LEGISLATURE TRICKED

Stripped of a certain degree of polite language and logical unwillingness to admit that they were misinformed as to the real purposes of the water district act, it would appear that the four legislators were tricked into sponsoring a foundling whose potentialities are somewhat appalling. And, having been once misled, Messrs. Johnson, Swing, Waller, and Jones may not be blamed for viewing the amended bill with continued suspicion.

It is doubtful that the radical $500,000,000 water and power act, so emphatically rejected by the people of California in two elections, contained more arbitrary provisions. In fact, the metropolitan water district bill in some respects goes farther than the $500,000,000 water and power act in its Socialistic tendencies.

Recital of a few of the more drastic articles in the Socialistic scheme as originally drawn, will suffice to show the dangerous purposes of the real authors of the bill.

From Metropolitan Water District of Southern California, *The Metropolitan Water District of Southern California Colorado River Aqueduct* (brochure, c. 1931, Box 3, Frank Weymouth Papers; held by Special Collections, Claremont Colleges Library, Claremont, CA).

THE METROPOLITAN WATER DISTRICT OF SOUTHERN CALIFORNIA COLORADO RIVER AQUEDUCT
THE DISTRICT—ITS GOVERNMENT, BOUNDARIES, PURPOSE, POPULATION, AND FINANCIAL RESOURCES, WATER RIGHTS, SURVEYS, PLANS AND ESTIMATES, CONSULTING BOARDS, FUNDS REQUIRED, PLAN OF REPAYMENT, OFFICERS AND DIRECTORS

Nature and Composition of District

The Metropolitan Water District is a public corporation of the State of California, organized in 1928 under authority of the State Metropolitan Water District Act of

1927. It is composed of the following thirteen member cities: Anaheim, Beverly Hills, Burbank, Compton, Fullerton, Glendale, Long Beach, Los Angeles, Pasadena, San Marino, Santa Ana, Santa Monica and Torrance.

PURPOSE

The District was organized for the purpose of supplying its member cities with water for domestic and industrial uses and incidentally to provide a means of creating a water supply for such surrounding areas as may find it advantageous to join in the enterprise.

GOVERNMENT

The District is governed by a board of directors composed of at least one director from each member city, the voting power being distributed among the member cities upon the basis of one vote for each ten million dollars assessed valuation, with the provision that no one city shall have more than 50% of the voting strength of the board. The members of the board of directors are appointed by the executive officers of the member cities with the consent and approval of the governing bodies thereof. The District has authority to acquire, construct and operate a water works system, do all the things incidental to these functions, and sell water and levy taxes to provide funds for carrying on its business and for paying interest and principal of any bonded indebtedness.

ENVIRONMENT

The region within which the cities of the Metropolitan Water District are situated embraces the fertile plain surrounding the city of Los Angeles and extending to Redlands on the east and Newport Beach on the south. There are 2,200 square miles or 1,400,000 acres of first class habitable lands within this basin. Citrus fruits and semitropical vegetation grow luxuriantly. The region is very attractive as a place of residence and as the site of an intense industrial development. Labor is plentiful at moderate prices and foodstuffs are abundant. The oil fields of Southern California provide an abundant and cheap supply of fuel, and the Los Angeles harbor is an open door to the raw material markets of the world.

FINANCIAL RESOURCES

The District at the present time has no bonded or other indebtedness. Current operating expenses are met by a small tax levy. The total population of the thirteen member cities in 1930 was 1,665,833, and the total assessed valuation was $2,410,610,355 distributed as shown in the accompanying table.

POPULATION AND ASSESSED VALUE OF DISTRICT

City	Population, 1930	Assessed Value, 1930
Anaheim	10,995	$8,188,260
Beverly Hills	17,429	64,448,585
Burbank	16,662	25,951,035
Compton	12,516	10,702,885

Fullerton	10,860	12,666,140
Glendale	62,736	73,472,110
Long Beach	142,032	189,399,040
Los Angeles	1,238,048	1,788,834,265
Pasadena	76,086	114,574,405
San Marino	3,730	14,885,855
Santa Ana	30,322	21,982,015
Santa Monica	37,146	59,618,185
Torrance	7,271	25,887,575
Total	1,665,833	$2,410,610,355

The above figures are for the cities now in the District. These assessed valuations do not include the value of solvent credits, stocks, bonds, notes, etc., the operative property of public utilities and the property of public corporations exempt from taxation. The Colorado River aqueduct is the only source of additional supply for the entire basin previously described and is being so designed that all potential demands can be supplied up to the limit of its capacity. The population of the basin in 1930 was 2,491,000 and its assessed valuation was $3,581,261,000.

PAST AND PREDICTED GROWTH

This region has experienced a remarkable era of expansion during the past few decades. Growth has been particularly rapid since about 1910. There is every reason to expect that development will continue until the natural resources of the region are absorbed. Past and estimated growths are as shown on the accompanying table.

PAST AND PREDICTED GROWTHS

(U.S. Census and Assessment Records)

| | Present Member Cities | | Entire Basin | |
Year	Population	Assessed Value	Population	Assessed Value
1890	62,322	140,540		
1900	123,294	235,820		
1910	391,595	284,000,000	668,038	529,992,000
1920	737,483	668,000,000	1,085,000	995,206,000
1930	1,665,833	2,431,397,2250	2,491,000	3,581,261,000

PREDICTED FOR FUTURE

1940	2,500,900	3,646,518,000	3,717,000	5,345,000,000
1950	3,360,200	4,933,826,000	4,940,000	7,104,000,000
1960	4,119,500	6,074,114,000	5,935,000	8,535,000,000
1970	4,824,300	7,131,520,000	6,860,000	9,865,000,000
1980	5,310,500	7,921,031,000	7,525,000	10,821,000,000

PRESENT WATER RESOURCES

The region is naturally semiarid, the mean annual rainfall being approximately 15 inches. The mountain areas tributary to the basin are not large. Natural stream flow is limited and even with careful conservation is inadequate for the needs of the community.

The areas immediately outside of the encircling hills are arid and yield practically no runoff. It is therefore necessary in the development of the region to go great distances to secure the waters needed to supplement local supplies.

The present Owens River aqueduct of the city of Los Angeles, extending approximately 250 miles northward to tap the snow banks of the High Sierra, is capable of delivering 450 second-feet of water into the valley, or such smaller flow as may be available at the source of supply.

PRESENT DEFICIENCIES IN SUPPLY

The entire amount of water being developed and used in the metropolitan area for all purposes and from local and outside sources is a little more than 1,000,000 acre feet per year. This amount exceeds the average yield of the sources from which it is being drawn by an appreciable percentage. This excess of use over normal supply is made possible by the fact that much of the water is derived from wells driven into the immense gravel beds underlying the area, which were filled with water prior to the settlement of California.

Many of these wells have been over-pumped until they have gone dry, leaving their owners without a water supply. Unless this condition is promptly relieved, growth within the metropolitan area must cease and retrogression is inevitable. Some further outside source of supply must be made available. At least double the present supply will be needed within the readily predictable future.

THE COLORADO RIVER AS A NEW SOURCE OF SUPPLY

Opportunity for the development of the needed supply is being created by the construction, by the U.S. Government, of the Hoover dam on the Colorado River. There is available no other source of supply suitable in quality and quantity and the people of the metropolitan area have no alternative but to undertake this great water supply project. Fortunately, Colorado River water can be brought into the District at a feasible cost.

2
———

Harnessing the Rivers

The construction and operation of a great dam should never be left to the sole judgment of one man, no matter how eminent.
—LOS ANGELES COUNTY CORONER'S INQUEST, *1928.*

Don't blame anybody else, you just fasten it on me. If there is an error in human judgment, I was the human.
—WILLIAM MULHOLLAND, *1928*

As booster campaigns attempted to generate political support for huge new water projects, other planning went into imagining and reimaging gargantuan aspects of water infrastructure. Planners had to figure out if the projects were even necessary based on present resources and contemplated growth. If they were not, how much more water would be required, or how much flooding would need to be prevented, how much would such a project cost to complete, and how would it be paid for?

Engineers of the time had to design and build massive structures to last for many decades, if not longer. These engineers increasingly were seen as expert professionals in their field. In the heyday of the Progressive Era and after, they were admired for their technical contributions to the betterment of society. Many were touted as national leaders, even potential political candidates. The construction of the Panama Canal and other major water infrastructure across the globe raised the status of engineers to that of national heroes in their ability to control nature and put it to use for humankind.

Not all of the projects would be completely successful from a construction perspective.

Massive floods in Los Angeles County in the 1930s resulted in the questioning of previous flood control methods. The catastrophic failure of the St. Francis Dam, a component of the Owens River Aqueduct, in 1928 cast a pall on such projects for years. Leakages in Hoover Dam (formerly Boulder Dam) eventually demonstrated that such behemoths might not last forever. Severe climate conditions,

FIGURE 29. Los Angeles River flood damage in the second decade of the twentieth century.
Courtesy of the Los Angeles Public Library Photo Collection.

earth movements, and faulty construction methods can take a serious toll on the best-laid plans for heralded engineering feats.

· · ·

The question of whether or not a specific project was actually necessary is certainly part of the historical record. Do we need this? Why? When it came to controlling floods in Los Angeles County, almost everyone and every major group was on board. The chief question was not whether it should happen but, rather, how to pay for it. Should all county residents contribute equally, or should only those who needed the protection pay for it? Should Los Angeles shoulder the cost, or should it be distributed somehow equally or equitably across the many municipalities or jurisdictions through which the river flowed? The following 1914 *Los Angeles Times* story describes the early role of organizations in the campaign to support the county supervisors in creating an agency to bring flood control to the Los Angeles River.

From "Mammoth Undertaking Fathered by County" (*Los Angeles Times,* July 2, 1914).

"MAMMOTH UNDERTAKING FATHERED BY COUNTY.

FLOOD CONTROL PLANS ARE APPROVED AT REPRESENTATIVE GATHERING.

EXPENDITURE OF NINE AND ONE-HALF MILLIONS IS CONTEMPLATED—STATE
AND FEDERAL. AID WILL BE SOUGHT—TAX LEVY TO PROVIDE MONEY FOR INI-
TIAL WORK BEFORE WINTER FLOODS ARRIVE."

Los Angeles County put its hand to a $9,500,000 undertaking yesterday, when 230
representatives of municipalities, civic organizations, drainage districts, and private
interests met with the Board of Supervisors in Blanchard Hall, effected a permanent
organization, approved the flood-control plans of the board's advisory commission
of engineers, and authorized the imposing of a tax of 10 cents on the $100 to get the
work under way.

The amount that will be raised by this tax levy was estimated by Chairman Pridham at $675,000. This sum will be used under the board's direction to safeguard the
county against possible flood loss the coming winter and to carry out preliminary
work in connection with the larger conservation plan.

Eventually it is believed that the State and Federal governments and private interests will join the county in the work. This will mean, it is believed, an equal division
of expense. The Board of Supervisors was authorized to take such steps as it deems
best to secure the co-operation of these other interested parties. It is possible in this
connection that the State Legislature will be asked at the January session to erect Los
Angeles county into one homogeneous drainage district similar to that now controlled by the Sacramento River Drainage Commission.

ALL TOGETHER.

With the flood-damage last winter estimated at close to $7,000,000 the assembly
early manifested the desire to tackle the problem as one in which sectional interests
should be forgotten. The result was the organization of the Los Angeles County Flood
Control Association, with Chairman Pridham of the Board of Supervisors as president: A. W. Fry of Clearwater as vice-president; Secretary McPherrin of the Board of
Supervisors as secretary and Col. H. C. Hubbard of San Fernando as treasurer.

There were few hitches in the proceedings. One was when it seemed possible
that the resolutions would contain no provision by which money would be provided
for work this fall. This difficulty was solved when the special tax levy was provided
for. Another came when Supervisor Norton leaped into the breach, when things
were going smoothly, with an offer to "save you money." He suggested "gravel dams"
upstream, an idea which brought a storm of derisive handclaps and a reply from
Mr. Norton that "they are trying to irritate me, but they can't do it."

THE PLATFORM.

The platform of the organization is contained in the following self-explanatory resolutions, drafted by Percy H. Clark, H. Hawgood, a member of the advisory commission of engineers; T. P. Lukens and Levi Carse:

"Whereas the floods of the past winter have resulted in the destruction of property within the county of Los Angeles, estimated by an impartial board of engineers,

as a total direct loss of $7,000,000, of which the county lost $495,000 for bridges and highways; utility corporations, $2,275,000, and the city of Los Angeles, $500,000. Traffic has been interrupted, business disturbed and the taxable value of county property, according to records, reduced over $3,000,000, and

"Whereas, a direct benefit to the county lies in the maintenance of the public welfare, [and]

"Whereas the average interval of time between those destructive floods has been approximately eight years during the past ninety years, and

"Whereas the rapidly increasing values of property in this county will cause greater damage in future years, and

"Whereas, as improvements are made and property values are increased, it becomes more difficult with each year's delay, to obtain necessary rights of way, and

"Whereas, supine indifference and lack of energy to meet these flood damages is not in harmony with the successful achievement of this county.

"Therefore, be it resolved, that the Board of Supervisors of Los Angeles county be requested by this convention to adopt an aggressive and constructive policy to control these flood waters along the following lines:

"First—The Control of the flood waters of the county, should be vested in a centralized authority, and should be in accordance with a comprehensive plan embracing the entire county.

"Second—No flood or storm water control construction or structure for waterways should be permitted that are not in accordance with the adopted general plan and approved by this authority.

"Third—The adopted plan should include consideration of the following essential physical features: (a) Prevention of overflow and erosion; (b) Reduction of the silt and debris of the flood waters, especially in the harbors; (c) The maintenance of the underground water supplies by spreading of flood waters on the debris cones; (d) The construction of such small mountain reservoirs as will minimize the flood peaks and incidentally increase irrigation water supplies; (e) Co-operation in protecting the forest cover in the mountains against fire and also by reforestation in the mountains, to restrain the floods and debris resulting from flood erosion.

"Fourth—The cost of the work should be distributed according to benefits, to civil divisions of the government and private interests. The division of these costs should include the Federal government because of its relation to navigation in the harbors, and the State, because of the general public welfare, and the county, because of damage to roads and bridges. There is precedent for expenditures by all these interests, for reclamation work of this class in California, as evidenced in the Federal reports of and appropriations for the California Debris Commission, consisting of army engineers, and for the State Flood Control Board, in accordance with acts of Congress and of the California State Legislature. Therefore, the Board of Supervisors is requested to have a careful investigation made by their legal and engineering advisors of these State and national acts, with a view of preparing necessary bills for submission to the United States Congress and the California Legislature. The county of Los Angeles should also, for similar reasons, contribute from its funds for the construction and maintenance of these works. We also recommend that the Board of Supervisors, by direct tax, shall raise such sums as they may deem necessary for immediate use, while the other provisions of these resolutions are being consummated.

"Fifth—There is precedent for diverting the flood waters out of the harbors. The San Diego River has been diverted into False Bay and the Calaveras River has been diverted from the Stockton Harbor, both at Federal expense. The diversion of the San Gabriel and Los Angeles Rivers from the San Pedro–Long Beach Harbors should be made at Federal expense.

"Sixth—It is to the public interest that the main rivers and their principal tributaries should have publicly owned and controlled channels. Near the canyon mouths ample publicly-owned areas should be provided on which the flood waters should be held and spread by an organized public effort. This will not only involve a large initial expense, but also persistent maintenance, with provisions for fighting menacing floods resembling that provided by the Federal Forest Reserve for fighting fires. The cost of these main flood channels should be widely distributed. After the adoption of the proposed general plan by the Supervisors, the local storm protection districts should be encouraged to proceed with their construction works in accordance therewith, provision being made for credits for the same in the event of the adoption of co-operative general legislation.

"Seventh—The Board of Supervisors is requested to immediately have surveys made, defining the necessary rights of way for flood channels, including the protection of the harbors, for areas on which flood waters should be spread for absorption, and for determination of available reservoir sites for storage purposes. Field examination should also be made to determine all areas that have been menaced, as well as injured by the floods of the past season, in order to properly define the outlines of the district to be benefitted by these proposed reclamation works. Complete surveys and information should be obtained, upon which may be based the definite plan and estimate, which should be sufficiently comprehensive in its scope to properly present to the engineering officers of the Federal government and those of the State of California, for the purpose of seeking co-operation by appropriation for the construction of these works.

"The Board of Supervisors should promptly initiate all necessary proceedings looking towards the adoption of the final plans and organization."

· · ·

Did Los Angeles really need another source of water in the early 1900s? Boosters said yes (loudly), while many opponents believed the Los Angeles River could provide enough water, at least for the near future. The city's engineers argued that the municipality was reaching its limit. If the population was to expand, more water would have to be imported from a second major source. This excerpt from the 1905 report of the city's Board of Water Commissioners presents the case for more water based on past usage, present resources, and projections for the future.

From Los Angeles Board of Water Commissioners, *Annual Report of the Board of Water Commissioners for the Year Ending November 30, 1905* ([Los Angeles: Los Angeles Board of Water Commissioners, 1905], 20–24).

UNDERGROUND WATERS BEING DEPLETED

The importance of the underground water supply in Southern California being recognized by the U.S. Geological Survey, Mr. W. C. Mendenhall, Geologist, was detailed to this work. The results already obtained by Mr. Mendenhall demonstrate the value of the investigation carried on by his department. The following data relative thereto has in large part been collected by him. Nearly every well south of the Sierra Madre Mountains has been inspected and the elevation of its water plane together with its output has been ascertained. The records in almost every case demonstrate the general lowering of the underground waters and the decreasing of the areas of the artesian basins.

In 1898 there were 375 square miles of valleys south of the Sierra Madre Mountains from which artesian waters could be obtained. In six years this area has decreased 33 1/2 per cent and in addition to the decrease of area there has been a very material decrease in the flow from the wells within the present limits of the basins. Numerous individual instances could be cited, but one or two perhaps will suffice. A well just above San Bernardino, when completed in June, 1892, flowed five million gallons per day. It has decreased 95 percent in output in six years. The famous Bouton well near Bixby, bored in 1899, yielded about four million gallons per day. On May 13, 1903, this well only flowed at the rate of 823,000 gallons per day, a decrease of 80 per cent. Almost every locality has numerous records of wells which once flowed, then ceased, and in which the water now stands many feet below the top of the casing. The former perennial streams of our lower valleys originated largely in certain cienegas which denoted artesian basins. The falling off of the flow from the artesian wells has been followed by a notable decrease in the surface output of those streams leading from the cienegas. Take the San Bernardino Basin as an illustration. The records of the Geological Survey show that in September, 1898, the surface flow, rising from the gravel beds above Colton, was 78 cubic feet per second or 3900 miner's inches. In five years the surface flow has decreased to 46 second feet or 2300 miner's inches, a falling off of over 40 per cent.

The statement that the streams of Southern California, rising from the gravel beds, may eventually be decreased to such an extent that there will be no surface flow except during torrential storms, is not intended as pessimistic, but the seriousness of the situation as it exists today and the results of various investigations should be faced.

The governing factor in the location of the Southern California towns was the proximity of perennial waters. An abundant water supply is absolutely essential to the progress and expansion of both city and suburban life. That this fact was recognized by the Mission Fathers is clearly demonstrated[,] and the growth of the towns of Southern California has been in almost every case directly proportional to the abundance or scarcity of its water supply.

While the artesian basins have been decreasing in area and output, a general lowering of the water plane throughout all Southern California has been taking place. This is of course more pronounced in some localities than in others, depending on numerous natural causes, as, proximity to stream channels from which the gravel voids are filled, porosity of soils, relative location in basin, whether at its upper or lower rim, etc. The Government records show many instructive examples of the lowering of the water plane. A few citations here of wells which are not exceptions but merely general in character, may be interesting. The water in the Johnson well, located north of the city of San Bernardino, has lowered from fifteen feet six inches below the ground surface in June, 1899, to forty-five feet below in June, 1904. In one well near San Dimas the water plane has fallen 65 feet in four years. In the well of J. B. Neff of Anaheim in March, 1898, the water stood 23 feet below the surface of the ground, and on August 1, 1905, it was 52 feet 7 inches. The Williams well near San Bernardino flowed over the casing in 1893, while last year the water stood 38 feet below the surface of the ground. Many instances similar in character could be cited but those noted above will suffice to demonstrate the seriousness of the depletion of our underground supply. Almost every rancher who has been depending on pumped water for the vitality of his orchards has realized the decline in the plane of saturation not so much because of the decrease in volume of the supply but because of the increased cost.

CITY DEMAND AND SUPPLY.

It has become fully recognized, by students of this problem, that the limit of the present available water supply for the city of Los Angeles is being approached. This is also true of Hollywood and Pasadena. This may be too strong a statement to readily accept, but investigations of the past ten years in connection with data previously compiled, so forcibly present facts that a conclusion differing from the above can only be arrived at by assuming that nature will in some bounteous and providential way come to our rescue. Should we have a series of wet years in which the rainfall is above the average, the necessary withdrawals may be made from the gravel beds without lowering the water levels, but even with an uninterrupted sequence of wet years the growth of our city and its surrounding territory if continued in a ratio at all similar to the years just passed, will demand all of the water which can be developed from our present sources, and that, without allowing a surplus for the recharging of the already depleted underground sources of supply. On the other hand, should nature continue her delinquency for another series of years similar to those of 1897–00 we can surely anticipate a shortage, unless all development and progress, both commercial and agricultural, cease. The third annual report of the Board of Water Commissioners of the City of Los Angeles, dated November 30, 1904, shows that there were three periods during the summer of 1904 when the water consumption of Los Angeles exceeded the supply by nearly three and one-half million gallons per day. The report further states that "it was only by appealing to the people through the press and otherwise, to practice the strictest economy" that the consumption dropped sufficiently to allow of filling the domestic reservoirs again. The same report

states that the city's supply was only endangered during the three extremely hot periods and that the minimum supply was equal to the maximum withdrawals at all
other times, but that the margin left after supplying the amount actually essential
for domestic use did not permit of any water for the Park lakes during that season
of the year. Again quoting from the report mentioned above: "In former years when
such heated terms occurred it was only necessary to make temporary drafts on the
surplus water that was usually used for irrigating purposes, but the whole flow of the
stream is now devoted to domestic use, and the zanja system abandoned. This caused
a great deal of hardship to many who had rich alfalfa fields and orchards within the
city limits, but they patiently accepted the inevitable and relinquished the rights they
or their predecessors had held for over a century."

Those were the conditions obtaining in the summer of 1904, and since that time
the city has added probably twenty thousand people to her population, requiring
under ordinary conditions of temperature and season three million gallons more
water each day; during the hot summer months this will mean an increased demand
of four million gallons per day.

• • •

Almost two decades after the issuance of the previous report, a board of three local engineers was charged with again examining the city's water-supply situation.
The board concluded that, based upon estimates of population growth over the
next thirty-five years, there would surely be water shortages unless new supplies
were found. Statistical models wrestled with three main questions: how many
people, how much rain, and how much groundwater should the city expect?
Although their population projections would prove to be generous, the three
engineers—Louis C. Hill, J. B. Lippincott, and A. L. Sonderegger—were sure that
another source of water would have to be found if the metropolitan area was to
grow and thrive.

From Board of Engineers, "Summary of Report on the Water Supply for the City of
Los Angeles and the Metropolitan Area" (August 14, 1924, typescript copy, 5 pages,
held by Special Collections, Claremont Colleges Library, Claremont, CA).

> Los Angeles, California,
> August 14, 1924,
> Board of Public Service,
> The City of Los Angeles.

GENTLEMEN:

Pursuant to your instructions, this Board of Engineers has investigated the present and future water supply which might be obtained from the Owens Valley, from
Mono Basin, and from local sources, and has estimated the future needs of the City
of Los Angeles and of the Metropolitan area considered as all of the Los Angeles

County south of the High Mountains. As requested, we have confined the report to a finding of facts.

The future growth of the City of Los Angeles and of the Metropolitan Area is dependent upon the water supply. Assuming a full supply, by 1940 the City will have about 1,720,000 inhabitants and the County about 2,740,000. By 1950 the City will have 2,180,000 and the County 3,270,000 population.

The available local supply for the City of Los Angeles is about 139 second feet continuous flow. In addition 400 second feet can be delivered by the aqueduct from Owens Valley during the driest years and leave 30,000 acres under irrigation in Owens Valley. It is assumed that adequate storage is provided at both ends of the aqueduct and pumping rights acquired.

The water requirements of the City within its present boundaries will absorb all of those supplies including return water from the aqueduct by 1940. If all Mono Basin water is added to the entire amount which can be conserved in Owens Valley after destroying all irrigation, and there is built a second aqueduct of 350 second feet capacity, then including the local supply, there would be available 920 second feet continuous flow or about enough for the City within its present boundaries for the next thirty-five years. However, the entire possible safe supply for the Metropolitan Area, including all local supplies in Los Angeles County, all of Mono Basin and all of Owens Valley water[,] is but 1315 second feet continuous flow and will only serve adequately the Metropolitan Area until 1933. By 1950 this area will require about 1870 second feet continuous flow of 555 second feet more than all possible available supply from local sources, Owens Valley and Mono Basin. If irrigation in Owens Valley is not destroyed and a second aqueduct not built the deficit will be about 900 second feet.

In 1905 when the City of Los Angeles determined to construct its aqueduct, it built it with a capacity not only adequate to care for the area within its boundaries, at that time, but also sufficient to permit of its expansion over 100,000 acres or more additional. It was this wise policy which had sustained the phenomenal growth of the City during the past twenty years. We are today facing a similar situation and it will be more difficult each year to obtain a large additional water supply.

Continued growth of the community coincident with the occurrence of a series of wet years might make a shortage of water unapparent. At the first recurrence of dry years, however, an acute shortage would result if an additional water supply is not provided.

CYCLIC FLUCTUATIONS OF WATER SUPPLY

California as far north as Owens and Mono Valleys is subject to synchronous periodic fluctuations of rainfall and stream flow. In the past, the periods of drought have averaged about eleven years.

In Southern California the water crop of dry periods is supplemented by underground storage. Sole reliance on surface streams is particularly hazardous for water users. The water supply must be gaged by dry years. Storage is required to regulate the excess flow of wet years. To base the development of a country upon the supply of wet periods will lead to disaster.

In Owens Valley the present drought is the most severe of record[,] but in Southern California that of the late nineties was worse. The Owens River is not subject to as great fluctuation in flow as other large streams south of the Yosemite. The estimates of available local supply have been based upon the dry period 1893–1904 and for the Owens and Mono Valleys upon the past nine years.

LOCAL WATER SUPPLY

The local water supply available in the Metropolitan Area during a dry period depends principally upon the ground water storage accumulated during wet periods, which becomes available in rising streams as at the Los Angeles and San Gabriel Narrows, or by pumping. The ground water reservoirs of San Fernando Valley, San Gabriel Valley, Southern and Western Coastal Plains and portions of Pomona Valley are very deep and of such capacity that over one half million acre feet, or a supply of 350 second feet[,] could be abstracted for two years with moderate pumping lifts. This enormous available ground water storage represents the accumulation of long periods. The permanent water crop is to be gaged by the average recharge. Most of these underground basins are now being overdrawn by the operation of hundreds of pumping plants.

The San Fernando Valley is the terminus of the aqueduct. Located along its periphery are some of the principal surface reservoirs for the storage of the winter surplus of aqueduct water. The valley itself is a great underground reservoir. The City has established its control of this water supply. The Los Angeles river in July, 1924, flowed 78 second feet of which 20 second feet was return water from irrigation in that valley. There has also been accumulated in the gravels underlying the valley an additional 100,000 acre feet of water from irrigation.

FUTURE POPULATION

The growth of the City of Los Angeles in the past has paralleled that of Chicago and probably will continue to do so for the next 25 years. The estimated population of Los Angeles is 960,000 at present; in 1930, 1,130,000; in 1940, 1,720,000; in 1950, 2,180,000; in 1960, 2,500,000. The estimated population of the Metropolitan Area is 1,400,000 at present; in 1930, 1,000,000; in 1940, 2,740,000; in 1950, 3,270,000; in 1960, 3,640,000.

Louis C. Hill, J. B. Lippincott, and A. L. Sonderegger

NOTE: One acre foot is the amount of water that will cover one acre one foot deep. One acre foot =. 325,850 gallons. One second foot = 646,320 gallons per day.

• • •

F. E. Weymouth, chief engineer of the Metropolitan Water District of Southern California, made a similar appeal for more water in this 1931 article for a professional engineering journal. Beyond the flood-control and hydroelectric benefits of Boulder Dam, then being built farther north on the Colorado River, Weymouth concentrates here on the need for a dependable water supply for the future growth of Los Angeles and the other ten cities in water partnership with the MWD.

FIGURE 30. F. E. Weymouth, chief engineer of the Metropolitan Water District of Southern California; William Mulholland, chief engineer of the Los Angeles City Water Department; and W. P. Whitsett, chairman of the Metropolitan Water District of Southern California, on a desert survey trip in 1931.
Courtesy of the Los Angeles Public Library Photo Collection.

Weymouth's population estimates and his conclusion that more water would be "urgently needed" proved optimistic, since little water from the Colorado would be taken by the cities when the Colorado River Aqueduct was completed in 1941. But it would be needed in the years to come.

From F. E. Weymouth, "Colorado River Aqueduct" (*Civil Engineering* 1, no. 5 [February 1931]: 372–376).

"COLORADO RIVER AQUEDUCT

ROUTE SELECTED FOR METROPOLITAN WATER DISTRICT REQUIRES PUMPING"

The Metropolitan Water District of Southern California is, in effect, a confederation of cities in the south coastal plain. It was organized in 1928 under the Metropolitan Water District Act of 1927, which authorizes the joining together of non-contiguous municipalities, or water districts, for the purpose of developing a domestic water supply. The district is governed by a Board of Directors composed of at least one director from each city, the voting power being distributed among the member cities on the basis of one vote for each $10,000,000 of assessed valuation, with the provision that no city shall have more than 50 per cent of the voting strength of the board.

Each city has the right to appoint an additional director for each $200,000,000 of assessed valuation without, however, increasing its voting power. The enabling act requires that the water be distributed among the member cities in proportion to their assessed valuations, the apportionment to be adjusted from time to time to conform to the growth of the various communities.

There are, at the present time, 11 cities in the district, having an aggregate population of 1,850,000, and an assessed valuation of two and one-third billion dollars. The act provides for the addition of other cities from time to time, and for separations. Three new applications have been recently submitted and formally accepted by the Board of Directors. Ratification by the people of the applicant cities is necessary before these applications become effective. Several other communities have expressed interest in the project. The area, which may be regarded as prospectively a part of the Metropolitan Water District, has a present population of 2,750,000[,] and this number must be considered in estimating future demands on the water supply.

PRESENT DEMAND FOR WATER

In 1929–1930 the City of Los Angeles used a total of 268,000 acre-ft. of water. A portion of this was developed from local wells; some of it was derived from surface flows in Owens Valley; and some was pumped from the Owens Valley gravels. No appreciable flows, subject to diversion by the city, went to waste and no water was accumulated in other surface or underground basins. In fact, ground water levels generally went down. In other words, the City of Los Angeles actually took more water from its sources of supply than was put back by nature. This does not mean that the city is actually facing an immediate water famine. There is still water in the underground basins available for emergency use, but the volume of underground water is not inexhaustible, and overdraft upon it cannot continue indefinitely. We are now, admittedly, in the midst of a dry cycle[,] and some relief may ultimately be expected through increased rainfall.

Rainfall records at Los Angeles, for a 50-year period, are shown in Fig. 1 [not included in this volume]. The precipitation has been declining, more or less gradually, since 1916. However, there have been many years with a lower rainfall than 1930, even in the brief period covered by these records. The 1893–1904 drought was more severe than the present one. It would be bold to assume that others, still more severe, will not occur in the future. It appears that Los Angeles is in a dangerous position as to future water supply, and it is evident that more water will be urgently needed by the time Colorado River water can be brought in.

ESTIMATED ULTIMATE DEMAND

The habitable area of the coastal plain is approximately 2,200 square miles, or 1,400,000 acres. The contemplated Colorado River Aqueduct, after allowing for losses, will deliver something less than 1,000,000 acre-ft. per year into local storage reservoirs or, say, 0.70 acre-ft. per acre. The Los Angeles Aqueduct, extended to Mono Basin, can be depended upon for perhaps 0.20 of an acre-ft., bringing the supply up to 0.90. Run-off from the 3,900 square miles of the south coastal plain may be counted upon to supply an additional 0.4 acre-ft. per acre.

Then the total supply, with all prospective importations, amounts to approximately 1.30 acre-ft. per acre. This is a gross figure, and with no allowance for losses in handling and distributing. As an irrigation supply, it is a modest amount, but as a domestic supply it is low, even for sparsely settled sections, and it makes no allowance for the heavy usage in congested and industrial districts. This allowance will probably be slightly increased by sewage reclamation and perhaps more notably by "return flow" from irrigation when a more bountiful primary supply is made available.

A proposed aqueduct capacity of 1,500 sec-ft., or 1,086,000 acre-ft.[,] per year at the point of diversion, was not selected by the above process of reasoning. But these general statements show that, although the region will not be overwhelmed by a surplus of water from the Colorado River Aqueduct, it will nevertheless be placed in a reasonably secure position for a time.

The amount of the proposed Colorado River diversion was arrived at by a study of predicted population curves, based upon past and present population trends and comparisons with the growth curves of other large and progressive communities, such as Chicago and New York.

From 1930 to 1980, the contemplated construction and amortization period, the estimated population increase for "Metropolitan Los Angeles" is 7,500,000. At the point of wholesale delivery, 1 sec-ft. of flow is sufficient for approximately 5,000 people. Therefore, according to these curves, the district will need the entire 1,500 sec-ft. of new water by 1980.

· · ·

Opponents of the Colorado River Aqueduct argued that engineers such as Weymouth exaggerated regional population projections, the methods for financing the project without imposing taxes, and other elements of the project only to gain public support for it. As reports of consulting engineers favoring the project appeared, critics countered the assertions point by point. A summary of some of the objections presented to the Los Angeles Chamber of Commerce by businessman John Treanor appeared in the *Los Angeles Times* in 1931.

From "Do We Really Need a $200,000,000 Aqueduct?" (*Los Angeles Times*, May 10, 1931 [Copyright © 1931. Los Angeles Times. Reprinted with permission.]).

"DO WE REALLY NEED A $200,000,000 AQUEDUCT?

BOTH SIDES OF ENORMOUSLY IMPORTANT COLORADO-PROJECT QUESTION; HUGE SAVING POSSIBLE, SAYS ANALYST"

Construction of the Metropolitan Water District aqueduct to 1500 second feet capacity will be a serious economic mistake, and the engineers who have estimated that amount of water as necessary or desirable are basing their estimate on error, according to an analysis of the Colorado River project by John Treanor, industrial and water expert, who declares that an aqueduct large enough to carry 500 second feet is ample for the requirements of the four counties (Los Angeles, Riverside, Orange and

San Bernardino) for the next thirty to sixty years, with full development of less costly supplies nearer at hand.

Further, he holds, such an aqueduct need only be of the "standby" variety, as no serious results will follow its temporary interruption, and he estimates it could be built for $50,000,000, or about one-fourth of the cost of the Parker Route $200,000,000 aqueduct which the Metropolitan Water District engineers have recommended.

Mr. Treanor's analysis of the water situation in the four counties is contained in a letter to Henry O. Wheeler, chairman of the Water and Power Committee of the Los Angeles Chamber of Commerce.

In his discussion he assumes that part of the water may become available for irrigation, or that temporary irrigation with a part of it may be possible, notwithstanding its legal restriction to domestic use. His argument, of course, would be even stronger against the present aqueduct plan if no irrigation use was to be considered. His references to irrigation, therefore, must be taken as assuming that irrigation use is legally possible.

Besides Mr. Treanor's analysis, the Chamber committee has before it papers by Chief Engineer Weymouth of the Metropolitan Water District and by A. L. Sonderegger, a consulting engineer, both of whom declare that the aqueduct as now planned is necessary. A summary of those papers follows the summary of Mr. Treanor's, together with a statement in reply from the Metropolitan Water District organization.

POINTS OF ANALYSIS

In brief, Mr. Treanor makes the following points:

(1) That no adequate engineering judgment has yet been had upon the water needs, present and prospective, of the community, but that the Metropolitan District engineers have merely been trying to plan for and locate correctly an aqueduct of predetermined size.

(2) That it has been assumed that a 1500-second feet aqueduct is needed on the basis of projecting fifty years into the future the growth-curve of this section between 1920 and 1930. This curve is not typical, he declares, because the rate of growth between 1910 and 1920 was below normal, while that between 1920 and 1930 was above normal, so that the curve constructed on those two points is exaggerated.

(3) That no irrigation users can pay the cost of Colorado River water except citrus growers, and that an expansion of the citrus industry at the rate figured by proponents of the big aqueduct is physically and economically impossible. The water will cost too much to make it available for alfalfa or other field crops.

(4) That there is no shortage of agricultural water except in Orange county, and the Whittier–La Habra district, and that an abundant supply for all the irrigation needs of this section may be had from reclaiming sewage, of which about 180 second feet are being wasted into the ocean at present from the Los Angeles area. This can be accomplished at much less cost than bringing in Colorado water.

(5) That without recourse to the Colorado all water needs, domestic and agricultural, for an additional population of 1,600,000, including 57,000 acres of

new citrus planting[,] can be supplied from comparatively near-by sources, with the possible exception of 20,000 acres of alfalfa in the Chino basin, which cannot afford Colorado water any way.

(6) That the population of the four counties will not exceed 5,000,000 by 1960, requiring an additional supply of about 180 second feet, for which the provision of 500 second feet, as he proposes, is more than ample.

. . .

Engineers, politicians, and boosters were concerned about how to pay for the Metropolitan Water District of Southern California project without creating new taxes, especially during the depths of the Great Depression. In this excerpt from a 1935 pamphlet, the financing scheme is laid out as a fact—no new taxes would be needed, just repayment of bonds, as part of any water bill. However, residents would eventually be assessed additional fees for the water to pay off the bonds and the continued operation of the aqueduct in the future.

From *Facts—Colorado River Aqueduct: Answers to Your Questions* (pamphlet, 1935, held by Special Collections, Claremont Colleges Library, Claremont, CA).

AQUEDUCT FINANCING

8. Are there any steps being taken to eliminate the necessity of collecting any taxes whatsoever during Aqueduct construction?

Yes.

(a) It is provided in the Metropolitan Water District Act that Aqueduct bond funds may be used to pay interest charges during the construction period, thus eliminating the necessity of collecting any tax money to pay interest charges on these bonds during the period of construction. Approximately three-fourths of the main Aqueduct construction work is already under way and contracted for, and the cost of this work is several million dollars under the original cost estimated—thus leaving a margin of bond funds available. The validity of the section of the Act just referred to has been established by a State Supreme Court decision.

(b) In the Federal Government's National Recovery Act it is provided that the Public Works Administration may give money amounting to 30% of the cost of materials and labor to such public works as the Colorado River Aqueduct. The District has applied for this grant of money. If this grant of money is received by the District it may be used to pay interest on outstanding Aqueduct bonds, and thus eliminate the necessity of making any tax levies whatsoever during the Aqueduct construction period.

9. What additional benefits will be derived from securing assistance from the P. W. A.?

Such assistance would immediately and greatly relieve unemployment in all the cities in the District. Under the District's present normal construction program 5,500 men were employed on the Aqueduct on March 15, 1935. If the Government grants the District's application, construction work on the Aqueduct immediately will be accelerated to the extent that several thousand more would be on the job within four months thereafter.

10. How will the cost of Colorado River water compare with the average cost of domestic water in the United States?

In 183 of the largest cities of the United States, the average maximum domestic rate for water is eighteen cents per 100 cubic feet. Careful studies of present and future water consumption in District cities reveal that if an average rate *even less* than this nation-wide average is charged, sufficient revenue will be derived to pay all bond interest, operating and maintenance charges entirely from water revenues. However, each city in the District has the power and right to decide how it is to meet its share of Aqueduct costs from water revenues, or whether it desires to meet these costs in part from water revenues and in part from taxation.

. . .

The adequacy of engineering and other facets of overall planning for water projects proved a common and regular concern. To devise a plan to prevent future flooding on the Los Angeles River and other rivers in the county, knowledge of flooding in the past one hundred years was deemed crucial. After the devastating 1914 floods, J. W. Reagan, a consulting engineer for the county and the U.S. Army Corp of Engineers, sent agents into the field to interview residents who had experienced past floods. With the help of "early pioneers," whose families had lived in the region for a century or more, the engineers assembled residents' knowledge of how the rivers had flooded and shifted in their beds since 1825. (See map 1 in chapter 1 for an illustration of the shifting river.) Their fascinating report would serve as the basis for planning and was also a compelling document of the social history of the region dating back to the Mission Era.

From U.S. Army Corp of Engineers, Engineer Office, "Los Angeles County Flood Control Records" (2 vols., 1914–1915, Huntington Library, San Marino, CA).

Mr. Wm. H. Workman

224 Douglas Bldg., L. A.

Mr. Workman remembers the floods of 1862–67–76–84 and 89 and more particularly about the Los Angeles river. It was commonly understood and talked of in early days by old Mexican people that the Los Angeles river flowed out through the southeast part of the city by Ballona and into the Santa Monica Bay until the flood of 1825. At that time the floods were probably the greatest for a great many years, when the river broke eastward into the San Pedro Bay. Many people here told Mr. Workman that this was the case. The floods of 1884 were perhaps the greatest in his memory. In that year immense amounts of wood floated down or were washed down from the mountains and supplied fuel for a long time.

The country from El Monte southward was immense sheets of water, and around Downey, Clearwater, Compton and Watts the country was covered with water for many weeks after the rain had stopped. The country down around Watts, Compton and southward was all willows, and especially near the so-called bed of the river, the willows were very dense. . . .

In early days the Los Angeles river had its bed where Los Angeles street now is; later it changed over to Alameda street, and in 1889 it changed its present course. The river was at all times very shallow until efforts were made to confine it to a certain channel, then it began to scour out as is clearly seen in the present channel.

Mr. Workman relates an incident of the flood of 1884, when Martin Aguirre, now a Deputy Sheriff, rescued a woman from drowning on upper Alameda street by riding his horse into the stream and bringing her out.

The floods of 1884 threatened his lands, and especially his apple orchards, but by keeping a force of men working for some little time he was able to divert the stream away from his place. One of the means by which he did this was to get a big gum tree and anchor the roots well into the solid bank, and then let the top drift down stream against the bank. This effectively turned the water and stopped the cutting. . . .

Judge G. Sepulveda, Room 1126 Merchants Bank Bldg.

Judge Sepulveda was seen at his office on Tuesday morning, August 11, as to the floods of his time.

His father was born here, and he also, and has some relatives here, but the ones who would know are dead. He says, however, that the Los Angeles River once flowed at the west side of the valley right up against the bank near the Plaza, and down along what is now Los Angeles St., and thence to Ballona Bay.

In 1825 there was a big flood and the channel of the river changed from the bank near the Plaza to the eastward and turned into the San Pedro Bay. . . .

Mr. Randall H. Hewitt, 529 Merchants Trust Bldg.

Mr. Hewitt was seen at his office this morning, August 31, by F. Z. Lee. He came to Los Angeles in 1876, and being connected with newspaper work for a great many years, attained intimate knowledge of the conditions of the country and the actions of the Los Angeles river since that time.

The year 1876 was a dry year and no water flowed below what was called the "toma" in those days, above the Downey St. Bridge, which is now North Broadway, where the boys used to go swimming.

The first big flood was in 1884. There were two sections of it. The first came down in the latter part of February, but did little damage. A great quantity of water fell and the country was very well soaked. Everyone thought the storm was over. The City Council was forced to take notice of the great danger the city was placed in should another flood come of equal magnitude or even greater. . . .

. . . It was decided to take some action to protect the city against overflow by the river[;] Don Antonio Coronel told them that there was a map in existence among some of the old early citizens which showed the river flowing along the bank which is now 6th St. from the southwesterly into Nigger Slough and into Playa del Rey and Ballona. Don Antonio said the map was practically only a sketch map but clearly showed the relative location of the hills and rivers; that succeeding floods had gradually forced the river eastward in its channel to where it is now.

In Mr. Hewitt's mind there is no doubt about the river having once flowed out through the southeast as there are plenty of indications to show it. . . .

Mr. Jos. W. Wolfskill, 540 S. Ardmore Av.

Mr. Wolfskill was seen at his home this afternoon, September 1, 1914, by F. Z. Lee. He claimed he had very little knowledge of the floods for he was never out in them. He has no memory of dates.

In early days the Los Angeles river had very low banks[,] and when the rains came the river was easily overflowed. The waters spread over the country and did little damage in those days. The water did not run so fast and did not cut so badly. The Arroyo Seco controlled the river at its junction because the fall of the Arroyo is so much steeper than that of the river. The flow of the Arroyo Seco against the bluffs has done much to turn the river eastward. Had this not been so, the river would be flowing where it used to, down near Main Street, as the banks at 6th down to 9th clearly show. The river has, no doubt, flowed into the Ballona in early days, but before this time.

Mr. Wolfskill's father told him that in early days the valley down towards Compton was almost impassible, for it was covered with marshes and lakes and there was a growth of willows and some large cottonwood trees. . . .

Mr. Geo. A. Wright, 466 P. E. Bldg.

Mr. Wright was seen at his office this morning by F. Z. Lee. Has lived here for 38 years and has witnessed some of the floods.

The flood of 1884 was probably the greatest of his time. The whole country was flooded. In Los Angeles the water came almost up to Main St. and he has seen the water three and four feet deep in Alameda St. These flood waters would cross over Main St. and flow to the southwest into Ballona Bay. This was also the case in 1889. This was no doubt the natural channel of the Los Angeles river in earlier times.

The country called the Cienega clearly shows this[,] as at one time it was all a swamp and always had three or four feet of water standing in the low places. The whole valley was marshy, swampy and covered with tullies [sic]. Now that the water has been kept out of there to a certain extent and the valley drained, people do not suspect that it is subject to floods.

The floods last year did a great deal of damage and in some cases people have blamed the railroads for some of the conditions, as the bridges held up the water until it flooded everything above them. The bridge or embankment would break and let a deluge of water down on the people below. Such was the case with the Laguna people last year. They are thoroughly sore about it. . . .

Mr. Jose Ruiz, Abila, P. O. at Watts.

Mr. Ruiz was seen at his home this P.M., Sept. 3, by F. Z. Lee. He is familiar with many of the events of the past sixty years, having come here from Santa Barbara when a child of three months with his family. He is now 68 years old.

When his father settled in the valley there were only four or five ranchers between Los Angeles and San Pedro. The land was covered with a heavy growth of blackberries, batamotes, willows, tullies, etc. There were marshes and lakes in several places around Watts and Compton. There were trails across the valley and between the ranches. Along the washes where the water stood or ran at times, the growth of willows and blackberries were especially dense. A man on horseback could scarcely get through.

In the early days, the old people used to say that the Los Angeles river flowed out through the southwest of Los Angeles and into the Ballona. The Cienega and Nigger Slough were low marshy places until only recent years[,] when efforts have been made to drain the country and to keep out the floods.

When he came here the Los Angeles river ran to the west of his place, and on down by the Dominguez hill. Later the river changed and flowed about a mile east of his place and again changed over as far as Tweedy.

His father has told him that he saw the valley from Boyle Heights to the Plaza one solid sheet of water. Mr. Ruiz has on his place some boulders, about the size of three-quarters of a cubic foot which came from a cellar dug by the Reyes family when their home was at 7th and Main. And just below the Reyes home, Mr. Reyes says there was a bluff fifteen to twenty feet high. Again, at about Alameda and Aliso St., he says there were high bluffs.

The 1889 flood covered the whole country and was impassable for several weeks. The rains set in and did not let up for about twenty days in one stretch. No one thought much of the floods in those days as they would only cover the ground and not wash to amount to anything.

Later when there was so much farming there[,] it began to wash more, and had there been as much rain last winter there would have been much greater damage. Some day big floods will come and then people will really be flooded. Nearly all the old people are gone who could tell about the floods in the early times. The young people do not care about these things, only spending the money coming off their land.

Mr. S. B. Reeve, Civil Engineer & Surveyor, 844 Title Ins. Bldg.

Mr. Reeve was seen at his office this afternoon, Sept. 1, 1914, by F. Z. Lee. He has been in Los Angeles County since 1878 and has been a close observer of the floods. . . .

When the first big aviation meet was held at Dominguez Field [in 1910], Mr. Reeve was chief engineer of the fields. He had a great deal of work to do in February. It had been raining a great deal and he was uneasy that he would not get the work completed. On one Sunday he had rushed his men out there to do some work and[,] along about noon[,] noticed the flood of water that was then coming down the valley. It spread out so much and looked as though there would be difficulty getting back to town[,] so he called his men off and caught an electric car to the city, which proved to be the last one in that day. The whole valley was one mass of water. . . .

Mr. Joseph Mesmer, 200 Franklin St.

Mr. Mesmer was seen at his office in the Jeffersonian this afternoon, September 8th, by F. Z. Lee. He has lived in Los Angeles since 1859 and from the nature of his father's business[,] which was that of a baker, and his connection with it delivering bread all over the "pueblo" at that time, many things are very vivid to him.

The first flood in Mr. Mesmer's time was that of 1860–61. This flood did little damage, but was remembered for the large amount of water that fall. The next flood and the largest of all, but not the most distinctive, was that of 1862–3.

During the winter there was a period of incessant rain, and on only one or two occasions was the sun seen and that for only a short time. The wet weather became so monotonous that on one occasion about a dozen men about town started out on a jamboree to drive "dull care away" by going about from hotel to hotel and from bar to bar, drinking and creating whatever fun they could. . . .

Mr. J. R. Ramirez, 812 N. Broadway.

Mr. Ramirez was seen this afternoon, Sept. 24, 1914, by F. Z. Lee, at his home.

Mr. Ramirez was born in Los Angeles in 1839. His great, great grandfather came to Los Angeles in 1786,—he thinks—and the descendants have lived on the old home place ever since. At the old home was made the first wine and brandy in Los Angeles.

In those early days up to 1825 the river flowed along San Fernando St. which is just below North Broadway at this point. In 1825, the floods were the greatest in the past 100 years. This flood filled the whole Los Angeles river valley from the bank between North Broadway and San Fernando Sts. to the S.P.R.R. yards on the other side of the river. This flood changed the course of the Los Angeles river eastward from its old bank, along Main St. to somewhere near Alameda St. Its entire course was changed to the south side of the city. The river flowed out through the Ballona Creek before this flood, but after this time it passed near the foot of the hills at Dominguez, and into San Pedro Bay.

There were other floods but none like that of 1825. There were big floods in 1832–42–49–52–59 and 62. The flood of 1862 was the largest since that of 1825.

In 1849 the river again changed its course from near Alameda St. further eastward to perhaps near its present location. It could change very easily anywhere[,] for there were very low banks and there was nothing to keep the water from going anywhere. The land was all swampy from Los Angeles to the sea. In the San Fernando valley there was a great marsh where the Lankershim ranch now is. There were few trees, some few Alamos and some willow. . . .

Mr. J. Frank Burns, 4315 Burns Ave., Los Angeles.

Mr. Burns was seen at Ball's Cigar Store this noon, Sept. 25, 1914, by F. Z. Lee. He came to this part of the country settling in the San Gabriel valley in February 1853, where he lived until 1860 when he moved to Los Angeles. He has lived here ever since with the exception of five years when he was back east. The flood of 1884 came during this period and he therefore did not see it. . . .

Mr. Burns talked to the old people of those days, one of whom was old man Pico, who was 93 years old at that time, but died eight or nine years ago. Another witness was 137 years old at that time. Both of these men told him that the Los Angeles river up to 1825 flowed along the high bank just east of Main St. down to about 17th St. and thence southwesterly into the Cienega and from there into the Ballona Creek and into Ballona Bay. . . .

The flood of 1889 came on Christmas day[,] when the greatest damage was done. Mr. Burns remembers this for he went down to help and did not get away for three days and nights. This flood carried out bridges and washed away the railroads and immense damage to the whole country. The Los Angeles river changed to the eastward below the city limits, broke into the Laguna ranch and joined with the San Gabriel river. The whole country was covered with water.

They should build dams to hold the flood water and build ditches along the hillsides to catch the water as it comes down the side. . . .

Romola Pico, 777 W. 16th St., Los Angeles.

Was seen at his home, 777 W. 16th St., Los Angeles, Sept. 22, 1914, by R. A. Borthick.

Says he went to San Fernando in 1859 when he was twelve years old[,] and lived and farmed in that section until about 1900. The first big flood he remembers was about 1861 or 1862 and there were very heavy and long rains[;] but he don't remember what section was under water in that flood. In 1867 and 1884 there were heavy floods and the country was overflowed much worse than in 1914. The section in through where Van Nuys and Lankershim is was badly flooded in 1884.

When the S.P.R.R. built their railroad they ran a dam or dyke from where they left their opening for the Tujunga waters, which is where the bridge on the San Fernando road closes [sic] to the town of San Fernando is, up to the point of hills to catch all the waters of both the Tujunga canyons and keep it from going down toward Rosco. Most of the dyke was washed out in the 1884 flood, but there is a part of it left. There was a mile or two of track washed out on the S.P. in 1884. The country was so wet in 1884 that a great deal of the grain could not be harvested in the valley.

Mrs. Lopez, San Fernando, Cal.

Was seen at her home in San Fernando October 5th, 1914, by R. A. Borthick. Mrs. J. T. Wilson, Mrs. Lopez' daughter[,] acting as interpreter.

Mrs. Lopez was born in Los Angeles in 1831, and came to San Fernando 63 years ago when she was married, on her wedding trip, and has been here ever since. She and her husband lived in an adobe house, which stood where the dam of the San Fernando aqueduct reservoir is now, and which was torn down to build the dam. She says the Wilson Canyon used to come down about where the S. P. pumping plant is[,] and on down and empty into the Mission reservoir, which was just a little piece above the Old Mission[;] and it was a live stream, and the Fathers used to store the water to irrigate with, and for domestic purposes for the mission.

In flood times, or heavy rains, the flood water would go out and overflow and spread over the flat section below the Mission, but there was no wash below the Mission[;] water just spread over the ground, and did no cutting. She says the Mission Fathers used to have a ditch from the Pacoima that led over to the Mission Reservoir, and they used to wash and scrub out the reservoir after a flood. In big rains or flood times there would be lots of trash and mud come down from Wilson's Canyon and fill the reservoir, so they dug a ditch from the Pacoima so they would have plenty of water. . . .

In 1858–9 there was a very big flood. She remembers the date and flood very well, because she went to Los Angeles to a christening, and looked the date up in the Family Bible, and it was between January and February, 1859. Her husband had just had a new carriage made that cost $300, and she was very much afraid they were going to lose it in crossing some of the streams. She says it rained for twenty days, and it was two weeks before they could get out of Los Angeles, and then they would not have tried it if they had not left some of their children at home, and were very anxious about them. She says there were several adobe houses just north of Cahuenga Pass that melted down and washed away in 1859. . . .

. . . Mrs. John T. Wilson says she drove from San Fernando to Los Angeles in 1884[;] and it seemed to her they were in water very nearly all the way from San Fernando, until they got across the Los Angeles River, and all down through the flat country where Van Nuys and Lankershim is[,] was a regular lake. She was going to Pomona, and was held up at El Monte—the bridge was washed out.

Mr. J. J. Morton, R.F.D. #1, Box 16, Compton, Cal.

Mr. Morton was seen at his home, October 9th, 1914, by R. A. Borthick. Lives on Main Street in Compton, between Long Beach Blvd. and Gibson St., on North side of Main St. Came to Compton in 1867 and has lived there ever since. Was elected Supervisor in 1876 and served to 1880. . . .

He says the 1867 flood formed a lake covering several hundred acres of land at least a mile and a half square, above and between Gardena and Los Angeles on the old Amstoy Place, and was known as the Amstoy Lake[;] and he thought [it] would always be there, but [it] disappeared, he does not know just when, but was there several years. . . .

In the early days of his time all of Watts and Willows were swamps, sloughs and tullies, and where the black soil in Watts is was a tullie and peat bed. He says some people used to cut and dry that soil and burn it. It afterwards dried out and they burned it off and cultivated it. . . .

He says when the big water came in December 24, 1867, it came in a rush and looked like a wall two or three feet high; the country was covered with mustard patches which a man could hardly walk through—higher than a man's head[;] and the waters gathered that and brush, and he claims thousands of snakes, squirrels and rabbits, and the next day the bed of the stream was practically level with the rest of the country[;] and the brush, mustard and sand went down to Rattlesnake Island, and filled up thousands of acres of sloughs, and connected the island with the main land.

He says they went up above Compton and tried to turn the water back into the old channel, but could not do so. . . .

He says the people imported a lot of carp about 1878 or 1879[,] and everybody that had a lake or pond got some carp and stocked them up and in 1889 was over-flowed[;] and their ponds washed out and their fish were carried down to Nigger Slough[,] and when Nigger Slough began drying up some years later, the fish commenced dying and made such a stench the supervisors had to hire men to clean them up and burn and bury them. . . .

In 1876 there was a bad flood. The water was so deep between his place and Compton or near Long Beach Blvd. that he had to put his feet up on the neck of the horses to keep them out of water. That flood was particularly bad in the section of the country near Lugo and a part of what is now Linwood [sic], and a portion of the Tweedy ranch.

Mr. Morton thinks the whole section around Compton that has been overflowed, and the most of it has been overflowed at one time or another since he has been here, has been filled from two to four feet. He says in 1867–76–84 and 89 the whole section of Compton was more or less overflowed, but says there were sections in one year that would not be under water and in other years the section that was overflowed would be filled up so much it was not covered in the next flood. He says in the 1889 flood the ground at the schoolhouse at the corner of Main and Gibson Sts. was not covered with water[;] and in the 1914 flood the water was about three feet deep.

In the 1914 flood the water got very nearly to Long Beach Blvd. but was very shallow, only about eight inches deep at his house[;] and the water was from his house east over past Clearwater and as far north as you could see and as far south as you could see.

. . .

The planning of the Owens River Aqueduct was hailed by engineers and others before and after the aqueduct's completion. One such story heaping praise on the project is this short notice about the Los Angeles engineers' successful struggle with nature in comparison to a similar project in New York. It appeared in *Scientific American* in November 1913, just days after local celebrations marked the completion of the aqueduct.

From "Completion of a Great Engineering Work" (*Scientific American* 109 [November 8, 1913]: 38).

"COMPLETION OF A GREAT ENGINEERING WORK"

The completion of the Los Angeles aqueduct, as described elsewhere in this issue, marks the successful ending of an arduous struggle with nature in its most rugged aspects of mountain and desert, and with powerful and subtle private interests for the possession of a priceless supply of water. The ten aqueducts of ancient Rome were marvels of engineering skill and durability; but their construction stretched

FIGURE 31. A scouting party of engineers in Owens Valley, 1903.
Courtesy of the Los Angeles Public Library Photo Collection.

FIGURE 32. Los Angeles Aqueduct survey team in Owens Valley, 1906–1907.
From the Frank Rolfe Collection of Negatives and Photographs in the Historical Society of Southern California Collection, photCL 400 vol. 12 (13), courtesy of The Huntington Library, San Marino, California.

over a period of five centuries, against the eight years that have lapsed since the Los Angeles aqueduct was first proposed, and the length and dimensions of the ancient Roman aqueducts bear no comparison with that of modern Los Angeles. The longest of the Roman aqueducts was 62 miles, while the Los Angeles aqueduct is 254 miles in length, from the intake on Owens River to the city limits of Los Angeles. The irrigation aqueducts of the Inca Indians of ancient Peru, one of which was 360 miles long, are among the wonders of the world, especially so when it is considered that they were constructed by a people uninformed as to modern engineering science and its methods, but these probably exhausted centuries of time. The 350 miles of iron pipe line, 30 inches in diameter, which conveys water across the arid plains of western Australia to the gold mining districts of Kalgoorlie and Coolgardie, is one of the triumphs of modern constructive hydraulic engineering; but this construction, although in a hot and waterless country, was comparatively level, while the Los Angeles aqueduct bores through miles of mountains of solid rock, crosses valleys on pillars of concrete in some places, and through huge steel siphons in others, and is of far greater dimensions than the notable Australian structure.

The great Ashokan aqueduct to supply the city of New York, now in course of construction, is the only modern hydraulic enterprise intended mainly for domestic and industrial use, that compares fairly with the Los Angeles aqueduct. The New York aqueduct crosses the Hudson over a thousand feet beneath the river bed, and it will furnish the metropolis with 500,000,000 gallons daily at a cost, including its various reservoirs, of about $165,000,000. The Los Angeles aqueduct has not much more than half the capacity, it is true; but it is about twice as long, passes through an incomparably rougher country, and its cost, when completed, will be less than one fifth that of the great New York enterprise.

. . .

Critics of the planning of the Boulder Dam charged that there were a number of deficiencies in the planning process; many of these charges, however, were based to some degree on the agenda of the critic. In this excerpt from a 1927 booklet printed by the National Utilities Association, author Frank Bohn summarizes the major points of criticism from a private-enterprise perspective in criticizing the early plans of engineers working for government agencies. The argument reveals disagreement among engineers concerning the present plan for the project; some of the details would change as the plans progressed.

From "The Engineering for this Project is Wholly Inadequate," in *The Boulder Canyon Dam: The Essence of the Swing-Johnson Bill*, ed. Frank Bohn ([n.p.: National Utilities Association, 1927], 17–18, held by Special Collections, Claremont Colleges Library, Claremont, CA).

"THE ENGINEERING FOR THIS PROJECT IS WHOLLY INADEQUATE"

Proponents of the Swing-Johnson bill often represent that no project ever came before Congress so well supported by authoritative engineering; that the plan for this high dam at Boulder Canyon is the result of the "composite" engineering studies of many leading engineers who have examined and reported upon the plan. The engineers most frequently alluded to in these representations are F. E. Weymouth, and other engineers of the Reclamation Service—a board of six Government engineers appointed by Secretary Work; engineers employed by the Los Angeles Bureau of Power and Light, Gen. George W. Goethals and Secretary Herbert Hoover.

An analysis of the facts reveals that these representations are grossly misleading, and that the facts are:

First: The engineering plan for this proposed dam at Boulder Canyon, and the estimates of cost and time required[,] are endorsed only by engineers of the U.S. Reclamation Service and in part supported by engineers of the Los Angeles Bureau of Power and Light. All of these engineers are employees of "interested parties." Cost estimates by Reclamation Service engineers admittedly are usually too low, and experience shows they are often only one-half or one-fourth of what they should be.

Second: The Board of six Government engineers appointed by Secretary Work did not recommend the construction of the dam proposed in this bill, and were only able to agree that as a part of a plan for development of the Colorado, a dam at or near Boulder Canyon of some height should be constructed at some time. They further strongly indicated the advisability of investigation of an alternative site—the one at Topock in Mohave Canyon.

Third: Two of these six engineers appointed by Secretary Work, one the chief engineer of the Federal Power Commission, the other representing the Geological Survey, criticized essential parts of the "high dam" scheme. One of these engineers definitely condemned it; the other pointed out that the outstanding fact was that insufficient data was available from which to arrive at any definite plan.

Fourth: Neither Gen. Goethals nor Secretary Hoover has examined the engineering plans or attempted to pass upon the estimates. Secretary Hoover has expressed approval of the general plan to construct a high dam, but has not attempted to pass upon the engineering. Gen. Goethals has suggested the advisability of another kind of dam and expressed doubt as to the strength of a masonry dam such as is proposed. He expressly stated that he had not examined the cost estimates. He therefore not only has not passed upon the engineering for this dam, but has advocated the construction of an entirely different kind of dam.

Fifth: Secretary Work, in submitting the Reclamation Service's plan for a high dam at Boulder Canyon, suggested to Congress the necessity for further study before appropriating Government funds for an undertaking of such magnitude.

Sixth: The only further study made of the Colorado development problem since the submission of the Reclamation Service's report to the Congress was made by the Geological Survey, which in 1925 published as Water Supply Paper 556, a full and careful study of the lower Colorado River and submitted a plan of development which did not include the high dam at Boulder Canyon. The chief author of that report, Mr. E. C. La Rue, Engineer of the Geological Survey, who has spent fifteen years studying the river and possible damsites thereon, and who admittedly knows the river better than any other living man, condemns the plan for the dam proposed in the Swing-Johnson bill, and does not recommend the building of any dam in Boulder Canyon.

. . .

The major civic and business organizations in the region generally approved of the overall planning of the Colorado River Aqueduct, believing that it would unquestionably spur population and economic growth. But concerns over the future population and water usage estimates used by the planners were brought up by civic leaders and some public officials as a threat to prosperity, especially during the Great Depression. One such criticism was raised by Los Angeles city councilman Roy Donley in 1933. In this short excerpt from Donley's sensational "Does the Colorado River Aqueduct Mean Economic Suicide for the City of Los Angeles?" he argues that the inflated estimates that would help win approval of the project would result in much higher property taxes that city residents would have to pay to finance water that would be used by others in the district. As it turned out, Angelenos would not need that water for some time to come.

From Roy Donley, "Does the Colorado River Aqueduct Mean Economic Suicide for the City of Los Angeles?" (typescript, c. 1933, 15–16, Box 1, A. L. Sonderegger Papers, held by Special Collections, Claremont Colleges Library, Claremont, CA).

> The engineers have accepted the figure of 2,500,000 as the present population of the Metropolitan Area, one half of this population being within the City of Los Angeles, and one half comprising the balance of the District. When the population of the District reaches the 3,000,000 mark, the population of the City will have increased 250,000 and the outside area an equal amount. There will then be required 50 CFS [cubic feet per second] of water for the City and 50 CFS for the outside area. The City will not need this 50 CFS because we already have that water available from our Inyo and Mono Counties' supply. The annual operating cost at that time will amount to $5,080,000.00. The annual sales to member cities ($0.04 per 100 cu. Ft.), will return a revenue of $630,000.00, leaving an annual operating deficit of $4,450,000.00. The annual fixed charges will approximate $11,000,000.00, making the net annual charge to member cities $15,450,000.00. The share which the City of Los Angeles will have to absorb will be $10,800,000.00[,] and a little figuring shows you that this will increase the annual tax rate of the City of Los Angeles 72 cents. How can you reconcile that with the cry for tax reduction? What effect do you think that will have on industries which may be inclined to locate with us? Do you believe that this city can continue to progress with such a staggering burden on its real estate?
>
> Not until the population of the Metropolitan area reaches the figure of 5,000,000 souls will we ever need a drop of water from the Colorado River. Not until the City of Los Angeles has increased its population 1,250,000 over what it now has, will it be necessary to use more water than is now available in Inyo and Mono basins, but

in the meantime we are paying 70 per cent of the cost, to provide water for the area outside the city.

We are packing an unnecessary and dangerous load until 1960 and for no good reason. Isn't it time to stop, look and listen? Isn't it time to review the entire matter, lest we awaken too late to avert economic disaster?

. . .

Engineers of water projects were hailed when the projects proved successful. Indeed William Mulholland, chief engineer for the city's water department, became a local hero when he completed the Owens River Aqueduct on time and under budget. With this engineering feat to his credit, he was prodded to run for mayor of the city in 1913. He refused. He then moved on to become a leader in the quest for more water, this time from the Colorado River. Mulholland received many glowing tributes in engineering publications in the 1920s and 1930s. This one, which appeared in *Western Construction News and Highways Builder* in 1933, traces the life and career of this "man of history and the maker of Los Angeles." There is no mention of the catastrophic 1928 failure of Mulholland's St. Francis Dam, a disaster that claimed about four hundred lives.

From "William Mulholland—Maker of Los Angeles—Pioneer in Southern California's Ceaseless Quest for Water—His Energy and Vision Have Made Possible the Colorado River Aqueduct" (*Western Construction News and Highways Builder* 8 [August 1933]: 330).

About fifty years ago "Bill" Mulholland camped near Upper Parker damsite, built a raft, and floated down Colorado river. Shortly after this he arrived in the little village of Los Angeles. Twenty years later, as the head of the fast-growing Los Angeles Water Department, he turned to the High Sierra in the eternal search for water—life's blood of the great Southwest. Hitching a pair of mules to a buckboard he sought—and found—in the shadow of Mt. Whitney in the Owens valley what then seemed to be an ample supply for several decades of progress in his rising metropolis.

In the ten years beginning in 1908 Mulholland overcame a succession of tremendous obstacles to complete, within his original estimate of $24,500,000, the 430 c.f.s. aqueduct extending 275 mi. from Owens valley to Los Angeles. That aqueduct stands today as one of the great hydraulic feats of the new century and has given efficient service since November 5, 1913, when Mulholland turned to his fellow Los Angelans gathered in San Fernando valley for the opening ceremonies and said, simply, "There it is—take it!" Thus on a highly dramatic occasion and with typical modesty he opened an era of unbounded growth along the south-coastal plain of California.

Demands on the Owens valley aqueduct and the city of Los Angeles' San Fernando valley well field as early as 1923 indicated to the visionary Mulholland [the] need for a large and dependable additional water supply. Turning again to Colorado river, scene of his investigations of 40 years before, he began surveys of the vast region

FIGURE 33. Los Angeles Water Department chief engineer William Mulholland.
Courtesy of the Los Angeles Public Library Photo Collection.

bounded by Boulder canyon on the north, Colorado river on the east, the Mexican border on the south, and the coastal plain on the west.

In December 1928 the Metropolitan Water District of Southern California was established and took over all engineering in connection with the Colorado River aqueduct. Frank E. Weymouth was made chief engineer of the district and under his direction the complex engineering studies on aqueduct location and design were carried forward. More than 50,000 sq. mi. of territory was surveyed and subjected to the most careful engineering and geological studies in the work of selecting the best, safest, and most economical aqueduct route. These studies, in 1930, led to Weymouth's recommendation that the aqueduct be constructed along the Parker route, with its intake above Upper Parker damsite, 16 mi. north of the little Arizona town of Parker. His recommendation was approved by a board of consulting engineers in the fall of 1930, and within a year the thirteen member cities of the district had voted a $220,000,000 bond issue for constructing the greatest hydraulic project in the known world.

William Mulholland was born in Belfast, Ireland, September 11, 1855, and educated at the Christian Brothers School, Dublin. At 15, with his brother, he answered the call of the sea and shipped 4 years before the mast. Eventually he landed at San Francisco—keen for adventure in America's land of promise. At 21 he bought a horse which carried him to southern California.

Destiny had determined that Bill Mulholland's career should be in hydraulics. His first job in Los Angeles was boring wells. He soon became superintendent of the water system of what was to become the west's largest city. In the next half-century in this capacity his sound judgment, unfailing sense of humor, and keen vision brought him well-earned recognition as a man of history and the maker of Los Angeles.

Three months ago, when the Colorado river aqueduct progress celebration was held at Cabazon to mark official commencement of construction, Mulholland spoke in these words to a friend and former employe: "I don't know whether I'm happy or sad. I'm the only one left of the old-timers who was instrumental in this project."

. . .

One component of the Owens River Aqueduct system was the St. Francis Dam, a 180-foot storage facility located about forty miles north of the city. William Mulholland had supervised the construction of the dam and deemed it safe when it was first filled in March 1928. On March 12 it collapsed, sending a flood of water to the Pacific Ocean. At least four hundred people were killed in the deluge, and property damage was in the many millions of dollars. Mulholland was held responsible for the catastrophe in the several resulting investigations. One of them was the Los Angeles County Coroner's jury inquiry, with its conclusions and recommendations printed below. In later jury testimony, a guilt-ridden Mulholland concluded (oddly) that "the only ones I envy about this thing are the ones who are dead."

From Los Angeles County Coroner, "Transcript of Testimony and Verdict of the Coroner's Jury in the Inquest over Victims of St. Francis Dam Disaster" (Case 26901, filed June 4, 1928, 2–5, Box 14, Richard Courtney Collection, Huntington Library, San Marino, CA).

CONCLUSIONS:

After carefully weighing all of the evidence, that has been presented, we have reached the following conclusions:

1st. The St. Francis Dam was defective due to the very poor quality of the underlying rock structure upon which it was built and to the fact that the design of the dam was not suited to inferior foundation conditions. The actual failure was caused either wholly or in part by these defects.

FIGURE 34. The last standing section of the St. Francis Dam in 1928.
Courtesy of the Los Angeles Public Library Photo Collection.

2nd. The construction of this dam, without having the design and foundation conditions passed upon by independent engineers and geologists, and without more thorough and systematic methods of design, supervision and inspection, involved two basic errors.

One of these was an error in engineering judgment in determining the character of the foundations at the St. Francis Dam site and deciding upon the best type of dam to build there,

The other was an error in regard to fundamental policy relating to public safety.

The responsibility for the error in engineering judgment rests upon the Bureau of Water Works and Supply, and the Chief Engineer thereof.

The responsibility for the error in public policy belongs to those to whom the Chief Engineer is subservient, including the Department of Water and Power commissioners, the legislative bodies of city and state, and to the public at large. It is a logical result of a set of conditions that the citizenship has allowed to develop and continue. This is the more fundamental error, for if proper safeguards had been provided in the city charter and in the state laws, making it impossible for excessive responsibility to be delegated to or assumed by any one individual in matters involving great menaces to public safety, it is unlikely that the engineering error would have escaped detection and produced a great disaster.

A sound policy of public safety and business and engineering judgment demands that the construction and operation of a great dam should never be left to the sole judgment of one man, no matter how eminent, without check by independent expert authority, for no one is free from error, and checking by independent experts will eliminate the effect of human error and insure safety.

The exemption of municipalities from supervision by state authorities in the building of dams involving public hazards is a very serious defect of the state law that should be corrected.

RECOMMENDATIONS

We respectfully recommend:

That the regulations governing the conduct of all municipal and county bodies engaged in building and operating dams be revised so that the construction and operation of all such dams will be subject to review by competent experts in addition to the regular executive engineering organization of the respective public bodies. It should not be left to the discretion of the Chief Engineer of such a body to submit such matters to experts, but should be mandatory upon the highest executive authority to employ thoroughly competent consultants that will not be subservient to the Chief Engineer.

That steps be taken to the end that all existing dams be thoroughly examined as to their safety by a board or boards of outstanding experts on the construction of dams.

That steps be taken to change the state law so as to place the building of municipal and county, as well as privately owned[,] dams under the jurisdiction of the state authorities.

The intent and effect of these measures would be to have three independent groups of experts pass judgment upon the design, construction and operations of dams and other structures which might involve hazards to public safety.

We, the jury, find no evidence of criminal act or intent on the part of the Board of Water Works and Supply of the City of Los Angeles, or any engineer or employee in the construction or operation of the St. Francis Dam, and we recommend that there be no criminal prosecution of any of the above by the District Attorney.

· · ·

The St. Francis Dam failure served as a wake-up call for engineers to take a critical look at future dam construction plans. One engineer, M. H. Gerry of San Francisco, took another look at the plans for Boulder Dam (also called Hoover Dam by 1930) and was convinced that it was unsafe, that its proposed foundation was faulty. In an article in *Civil Engineering* in July 1931, he compared its planning to that of the St. Francis Dam, a recipe for disaster. This summary of Gerry's article appeared in the *Denver Post* in July 1931, along with a response from U.S. Bureau of Reclamation chief Elwood Mead.

FIGURE 35. Hoover Dam (originally Boulder Dam) under construction, 1934.
Courtesy of the University of Southern California, on behalf of the USC Libraries.

From M. H. Gerry report on the safety of the Boulder Dam, as reported in Howard Blakeslee, "Hoover Dam Will Not Be Safe, Predicts California Engineer" (*Denver Post*, July 11, 1931 [Used with permission of The Associated Press Copyright © 2015. All rights reserved.]).

"HOOVER DAM WILL NOT BE SAFE, PREDICTS CALIFORNIA ENGINEER SAYS FAULTY FOUNDATION MAY RESULT IN DISASTER

CRITIC COMPARES BLUEPRINTS WITH THOSE USED IN CONSTRUCTION OF ST. FRANCIS DAM, WHICH COLLAPSED THREE YEARS AGO."

New York, July 11—Safety of the Hoover dam is questioned—is said to risk repetition of the St. Francis dam disaster—in the July issue of Civil Engineering, official publication of the American Society of Civil Engineers. The writer is M. H. Gerry Jr., a consulting engineer of San Francisco, and member of the society.

Hoover Dam, 727 feet high, the greatest hydraulic structure ever undertaken, still is in the blue print stage, but the design has been selected and the contract let, and the safety questions are raised about this design. The danger is said to be due to the rock upon which the dam will rest rather than in the structure itself.

This risk, the article claims, can be wiped out for an additional expense of 5 million dollars or less.

"It should not be forgotten," says the writer, "that three years ago the St. Francis dam, built by the city of Los Angeles, did fail, and without the slightest warning. Even a cursory examination of the plans now proposed will convince engineers that the Hoover dam is designed in accordance with the same school of thought and on all other similar lines.

"Like the St. Francis dam, it is deficient in gravity section when uplift is considered; it is curved in plan, on the same radius; and it is designed on the same general theory that some concurrent arch action will take place and thus overcome the limitations of the section—a theory widely disputed by engineers."

The statement, "deficient in gravity section when uplift is considered," means the dam's weight is insufficient to keep it from sliding with the weight of water pushing it from behind. The "uplift" is [the] upward push of water seeping under the dam, a push of tremendous power when the water is deep behind the dam.

. . .

Although the St. Francis Dam disaster cast a short-lived pall on dam construction, by late 1928 planning for the Boulder Dam passed the scrutiny of many engineers. One such group was a federal board of review appointed to analyze the design and construction features. These engineers approved the project as safe and feasible based on contemporary principles of engineering. Their report is described in *Engineering News-Record* in 1928.

From "The Boulder Dam Report" (*Engineering News-Record* 101 [December 13, 1928]: 868–869).

"THE BOULDER DAM REPORT"

Public service of unusually high type is reflected in the report of the Engineering Board of Review on the Boulder dam project. Responding fully, sanely and unequivocally to the queries placed before it, the report answers the major doubts with which Congress and the general citizen were disturbed last spring in the discussion of this contentious issue. It illuminates many points in which the main issue has been obscured. It accomplishes these things by means of broad and wise treatment of the subject—and herein the report is distinguished. All too often the work of a board or a committee exhibits less wisdom than is possessed by its individual members; in the present instance the excellence of the results embodies the conjoined wisdom of the group.

What does the board set forth? It gives full answer to four major questions.

First, it declares that the proposed 550-foot dam is feasible, is capable of being safely and readily built. Last spring, it will be recalled, suspicion was cast upon the feasibility of this great structure: at a time when bitter opposition was being centered upon the project on the score of power and of Arizona royalty claims, the failure of the St. Francis dam served as [the] basis for intimations that the proposed dam would not be safe, since, apparently no dams were safe. The report states positively that it is safe, whether placed in Boulder Canyon or in Black Canyon. The board takes an extreme attitude of conservatism in its comment on the design, and this cannot reasonably be criticized, for in a work of such character and magnitude it is indeed wise to purchase extra insurance. . . .

Second, it finds that the project will be effective to carry out the specific combination of purposes for which it was devised—namely, flood control, silt removal, flow equalization for most efficient water supply, and power generation. Here also important doubts were at issue, having been raised by many claims, based on small-scale facts and interpretations, that the combination of hydraulic functions is not practicable. Therefore, the clear-cut judgment expressed by the board is highly valuable. Here again a most conservative attitude is taken. The board rates the total flow lower, and the possible flood flow higher, than heretofore estimated—a sound procedure in a review by an appellate tribunal of a stream having such limited records and such picturesquely varied phenomena as the Colorado. The board's figures may not be nearer right than those previously calculated, but they are on the safe side.

Third, it concludes that the canal into the Imperial Valley can be built and maintained successfully, contrary to what had been claimed by many critics.

Fourth, it holds that the power byproduct of the dam is needed and is valuable, and that the project will pay, after due deduction (which, as we understand the past proceedings, has previously been contemplated) of flood-protection charges and the cost of the Imperial Valley canal. Significant and unreserved is the board's statement that the near-by territory has a power demand large enough to absorb the output of the project. This verdict sweeps away most of the background of the antagonism displayed by some of the utility interests—though the most farseeing have long appraised the situation in a more progressive light.

Several auxiliary questions are also disposed of by the report, but these four are of outstanding moment. They are sufficient to strip the project of much of the doubt in which it has been veiled and to place the central issue fully and fairly before Congress.

The board confined itself to the questions which it was instructed to answer, and therefore it did not touch many of the sore points of the Boulder dam case. But it is for Congress to decide whether this great, costly and far-reaching enterprise of controlling a menacingly wild river for the protection and development of the Southwest is a proper and desirable national function; to decide, among other things, whether the Colorado River compact is a secure basis for the utilization of the water; to determine how the inevitable involvement of power production in the project shall be dealt with; whether the Imperial Valley canal is a constructive method of improving the dangerous status of water supply on the Mexican border; whether it is best to allot the stored water by states or to leave it subject to established doctrine of beneficial appropriation under the remarkable circumstances surrounding the use of the lower Colorado; and whether the insistent claims of Arizona for power royalties ought to be recognized.

These and related questions were not before the board, and they would have been dangerous obstacles to a clear and firm disposal of the question specifically placed before it. That the board kept its studies and judgment free of these complications is a matter for sincere congratulation.

3

Rivers in Nature

And at last the drop that fell like a snowflake upon the Sierra's crest and set out to find its home in the sea, shall be taken up from beneath the ground by a thirsty rootlet and distilled into the perfume of an orange blossom in a garden of the City of the Queen of the Angels.

—ALLEN KELLY, *1916*

All of these large water development projects took a toll on the rivers and their watersheds as natural features were sacrificed for the greater good.

The treatment of the Los Angeles River by nearby residents has always been less than sympathetic. Used for drinking, bathing, and dumping over centuries, it has been polluted and cut into by irrigation and drainage ditches. Pollution has been addressed by municipal ordinances that have not always been effective. Frustration at the river's periodic and occasionally ferocious flooding spurred the city to try the Pyrrhic remedy of lining the riverbed with concrete to speed the water to the ocean; it also carried pollution and debris, which was then deposited at the mouth of the river, at the Port of Los Angeles. Lining of the river undoubtedly altered its ecology, as did the harbor complex at its mouth. Only in recent years have concerted restoration and revitalization efforts imagined a different river, a different riparian future.

The Owens River Aqueduct transferred so much water to Los Angeles from Owens Lake that the latter reverted to a saline bed with its drainage area battered by windy salt storms. Conflicts between Inyo County and Mono County residents and environmentalists and the Los Angeles Department of Water and Power continue today.

Ecological changes to flora and fauna as a result of the construction of Boulder Dam and the Colorado River Aqueduct became evident years after the completion of Boulder Dam. Both the additional water taken by the seven states for further development in the later twentieth century and climate change have depleted a significant amount of its supply. Concern about taking any more of it is still a major issue among the states and Mexico.

. . .

City officials and residents have long noted that the Los Angeles River is an easy target for abuse. Los Angeles archival records contain many reports by city officials documenting the trashing of the river by residents and businesses. One of them is this request by the city's park commissioners in 1912 for the city council members to view the "unsightly" condition of the river as it appears to visitors and "enforce reasonable restrictions" for its protection.

From "Report of Los Angeles City Park Commission" (Los Angeles City Council Minutes, February 13, 1912, 87:263–264, Los Angeles City Records Center).

The Park Commissioners reported:—

At a meeting of the Board of Park Commissioners held Monday, February 5th, 1912, I was directed to advise your honorable body as follows:—The official channel of the Los Angeles river extending from the mouth of the Arroyo Seco to the south boundary of the City, a distance of approximately four and one-half miles, with a width of approximately three hundred feet, cuts through the center of the city and is crossed by eleven streets and five railroad bridges. Both banks throughout its official course are occupied by railroads; in short it is an extremely prominent physical feature of the City for those residing therein, as well as for those entering and passing through. Its present condition is unsightly in the extreme; the bulkheads intended to restrain floods have either rotted or fallen down; and it is the dumping ground for the City. Large gravel pits are being dug, apparently without restraint or order, and teams engaged in removing gravel frequently haul back trash and dump it in the river bed. Members of the City Council are requested to observe these conditions when next in that vicinity. This gravel is the property of the City and is being taken in large quantities indiscriminately and as far as we know without permits. So much has been taken, that a general lowering of the river bed has resulted, and it has been necessary to lower bridge foundations and pipes, at a substantial expense to the City. The gravel is being mined in pits. A count has been kept by the Park Department, and it has found that an average of six hundred and seventy loads of gravel per day, Sundays excepted, is being removed and about twenty seven loads of rubbish per day, Sundays, excepted, is being dumped therein. It would be expensive and difficult if not impossible, ever to make the river bed a thing of beauty, but it is not necessary to have it so ugly and unsanitary.

If the honorable City Council will fix a charge of say ten cents per load for all gravel removed and authorize the Park Board to enforce reasonable restrictions for its protection, the Board would be pleased to expend the revenue so obtained in the parking and improvement of this unsightly back yard of the City. It appears to be a plain business proposition, that those who take the gravel should pay enough to keep the river bed in order.

. . .

Complaints to the city council about the condition of the river also include many communications from private businesses, organizations, and citizens. This 1926 letter from the representative of an Eastside homeowner group describes the river in his area as a disgraceful dumping ground that needs to be cleaned up.

From C. R. Vesper to Mayor and City Council, Los Angeles (January 26, 1926, File 984, Box A-274, Los Angeles City Records Center).

> To the Honerable *[sic]* Mayor And
> City Council of the City of
> Los Angeles California

At a regular meeting of the Board of Directors of the Hollenbeck Heights Improvement Assn. the following Resolution's *[sic]* were adopted, And your attention and consideration is as, ed *[sic]* in this important matter.

Whereas; The voting of the City Bonds, The Citizens of the EAST SIDE were lead to believe that with the coming of the aqueduct water supply that the Los Angeles River Bed would be Beautified by running water and the plantings of appropriate Plants and Shrubery *[sic]* along its banks.

Whereas The East Side is making rapid strides and is entitled to this improvement which will be not only a credit to the whole City but would favorably impress the Stranger within our gates.

Therefore Be it Resolved; That we the members of the Board of Directors of the Hollenbeck Heights Improvement Assn. Do deplore the present condition of the Los Angeles River Bed in its present disgracefull *[sic]* condition.

Resolved, That this Orgenazation *[sic]* do hereby request The Honerable *[sic]* Mayor and City Council too *[sic]* take such steps and employ such means to convert this River Bed into a place of Beauty rather than a Disgracefull *[sic]* Dumping ground and a Weed Patch that it now is.

And Be it Further Resolved That a copy of this resalation *[sic]* be sent to the Mayor the Los Angeles City Council and the City Press.

> C. R. Vesper
> Secretary

. . .

One of the main responsibilities of the chief engineer of the Los Angeles County Flood Control District was to make sure that the river channels were free of obstacles that would back up raging waters and contribute to flooding. In this note, chief engineer J. W. Reagan asks the Los Angeles City Council to order dumping to be stopped.

From James W. Reagan to Los Angeles City Council (October 7, 1920, Los Angeles City Council, File 2606, Box A-121, Los Angeles City Records Center).

City Council
Los Angeles, California

Gentlemen:

A dump of refuse is being made in the channel of the Los Angeles river upon the west side and immediately below the Macy Street Bridge. This dump is making a rather serious contraction of the channel at this place. It is true that at time of flood a portion, or perhaps all of it, will be eroded and carried away, but it is made up of such materials as will work a detriment and an injury to our channel below the city.

Respectfully yours,
Jas. W. Reagan
Chief Engineer, Los Angeles
County Flood Control District

. . .

A major report on planning for a parks system in the Los Angeles region by the nation's premier landscape architecture firm, Olmsted Brothers and Bartholomew and Associates, in 1930 incorporated flood control drainage for the Los Angeles River. Unfortunately, the overall plan commissioned by a private group of civic leaders proved to be too costly in the early stages of the Great Depression. However, it provides an insight into past development practices near the river and offers inspiration for those involved in the river's restoration.

From Olmsted Brothers and Bartholomew and Associates, Consultants, *Parks, Playgrounds and Beaches for the Los Angeles Region: A Report Submitted to the Citizens' Committee on Parks, Playgrounds and Beaches by Olmsted Brothers and Bartholomew and Associates, Consultants* ([Los Angeles: 1930], 14–16, 124–125).

PARKS AND THE DRAINAGE PROBLEM

To the experienced eye, the slopes of the land show approximately where water must concentrate in times of heavy rainfall. No matter how innocent it might look in dry weather, low land must always be far less valuable for building purposes than other land. But the lowlands may be just as good as any other for providing spaciousness of open scenery for parks and parkways; and it ought to be relatively cheap to acquire. Because of the innocent look it has in dry weather, it is not as cheap as it ought to be. Between floods it looks pretty good for building purposes to those who never saw what storm water can do in this country. Unsuspecting purchasers, victims of their own ignorance, will fall into the traps laid for them by the sharp practice of ruthless promoters, and such lands will be cut up, sold, and occupied. Unfortunately, the burden of such a wrong development does not fall on the purchaser alone, and scarcely ever on the vendor, but most heavily on the community at large. There is, of course, a remedy, but it requires vision and vigor to apply it. Remedial legislation might prevent further mistakes and correct those of the past.

To sum up this vexatious matter: The community is confronted with four possible courses:

First, and best, police regulation can be adopted to prevent costly improvements in floodways unless and until adequate spaces have been set apart for handling the maximum floods and the floods have been confined to them by permanent channels, reservoirs, and reserved areas for percolation into the ground. The cost would thus be fairly divided between the community at large and the owners of land more or less subject to flooding. Such a policy would not only be a direct financial benefit to the community, but would indirectly prevent the sharp practice above mentioned and stop the ill-directed spread of the population. It would also open the way to an economical purchase of park lands in the very areas where nothing else is so clearly practicable.

Second, the community can purchase such lands for park and flood-control purposes, while still vacant, but at speculative prices, that are high because based on the cupidity of speculators unrestrained by police regulations.

Third, the community can permit the lands to become built up, and periodically spend large sums to repair recurrent flood damage.

Fourth, after long delay, the community can, through heavy expenditure, permanently remove the flood menace by the purchase and destruction of costly improvements.

These are, of course, primarily flood-control and water-conservation problems; but there are many opportunities for combining with them, at little extra cost, parks along natural drainage lines on lands relatively cheap, and extensive enough for recreation purposes. Such land would only have to be acquired once, yet would serve a double purpose—flood-control use and park use—not conflicting but positively beneficial to each other. Especially would this be true of the land acquired as a margin of safety; the open land skirting the chief flood-control area which prudence would include in the purchase.

Where flood control alone is dealt with in computing the size of anticipated floods, there is a natural tendency to curtail the area of land to be acquired in this speculative market. Such curtailment is likely to reduce the factor of safety beyond the danger point. Such a policy defeats itself. It compels large outlays for costly construction on narrow rights of way which would not be necessary on wider rights of way. The combination of parks with flood-control necessities is frequently possible, and wherever practiced it not only will yield a double return on the investment of land but also may lead to *an ampler and better solution of both problems at a much lower cost of construction than either would separately pay* [italics in original]. . . .

The most serious question in any plan for improvement will necessarily be that of providing satisfactory and effective revetments or other forms of river control without seriously injuring the landscape value of the river bed. The prospect of a dam in the mountains to control the river offers a possibility of materially reducing the size of revetments required.

The river banks offer opportunities for special types of tree growth and special effects of foliage with cottonwoods, sycamores, willows and poplars, wild grapes and even sweet gums and sour gums. The already interesting foliage masses can be kept and made a striking feature of the district instead of giving way to an ugly vacant channel.

At the northerly end on the east bank is the old Pio Pico Adobe House, owned by the State, that should be included within the parkway reservation.

54. Lower Los Angeles River Parkway

From Long Beach northward to the Rio Hondo at South Gate the Lower Los Angeles River offers much the same problem as the Lower San Gabriel. Below Los Cerritos the river has already been confined between revetments 300 feet apart[,] and commercial use of the edges has been encouraged and made possible so that parkway construction of an interesting character would be difficult and costly if attempted, but above there where a right of way 400 feet or 500 feet wide is needed for flood control a width of 1,000 feet or so should be acquired, and above Center Street where the channel is broad and meandering a width of 1,500 feet or so in places seems desirable.

• • •

The impact of nature on urban growth sometimes takes the form of devastating floods; 1938 floodwaters roared through the Los Angeles Basin with particular fury. In their wake, flood control engineers studied what could and should be done next, contemplating, for instance, a comparison of historical rainfall totals against 1938 figures. In order to prevent another such catastrophic flood, the engineers decided to capture the floodwater and force it quickly to the Pacific Ocean by lining the riverbed in concrete.

From M. F. Burke, hydraulic engineer, "Flood of March 2, 1938" (Los Angeles County Flood Control District, May 20, 1938, Box 18, Los Angeles County Public Works Department Technical Library).

INTRODUCTION

On March 2, 1938, Los Angeles County experienced a major flood which equaled or exceeded any previous flood of record. A preliminary survey made shortly after showed a toll of known dead of 113 persons and an estimated damage amounting to forty-five million dollars.

Because future planning must be based in large part upon past records, and because the Los Angeles County Flood Control District is specifically organized for the business of planning Flood Control and protection works, the present report is compiled. It presents factual data on rainfall, runoff and debris movement as far as these data are available at the present time, and makes comparisons with past and anticipated storms and floods. It is essentially a compilation and preservation of records, rather than a solution to the problems arising. Only the obvious comparisons are drawn and speculation reduced to a minimum.

SUMMARY

Meteorological conditions previous to and during the storm were not unusual, but may be expected to occur, and have occurred, several times each year since the

District has engaged in meteorological analysis and forecast. From a meteorological point of view, worse conditions are possible and could be expected to produce a storm more intense and of longer duration than that which occurred from February 27 to March 4, 1938.

The total rainfall during the storm varied according to location in the County, ranging from seven inches near the ocean at Long Beach to a maximum of thirty inches on the face of the San Gabriel mountains and decreasing to about four inches in the desert near Lancaster. As far as records are available, this storm total about equaled the rainfall during the storm of December 1922, and exceeded all other storms during known flood periods. The maximum day's rainfall exceeded previous days' maxima during flood periods by about twenty per cent. As an average, the maximum day's rainfall had a probable recurrence frequency of sixty-five years. . . .

The runoff peaks for the large catchment areas equaled or exceeded any known peaks during previous floods and in some cases, approached the computed capital flood peak based on a fifty year rainfall frequency. In the smaller catchment areas, the present flood peaks have been exceeded by previous records, notably in the storm of New Year's, 1934. For these small drainage areas, the present flood peaks were only small percentages of the peaks computed for the capital flood. This is believed to be a direct result of the subnormal short time rainfall intensities experienced during the present storm. . . .

Even though the present storm may be considered the maximum of record, the actual areas subjected to inundation and flooding by water escaping from regular stream channels is less than was expected from a flood of this magnitude. This may be largely attributed to the channel protection work recently accomplished, and to the peak reduction effected by regulating reservoirs. . . .

COMPARISON OF RAINFALL ON MARCH 2ND WITH DAILY AMOUNTS HAVING A PROBABLE FREQUENCY OF 50 YEARS AS DETERMINED IN 1929

In the area bounded by the Santa Monica mountains, the Whittier Narrows, the Puente Hills and eastern County boundary, the March 2nd rainfall generally exceeded the 50 year storm rainfall. In the vicinity of Torrance the two were equal, while in the vicinity of Vermont Avenue and Santa Monica, the current storm exceeded the 50 year value by about an inch. . . .

As a summary, it may be said that for the drainage areas of the Los Angeles River, San Gabriel River and Ballona Creek, and for the Santa Monica mountains, the rainfall for March 2 exceeded, in general, the computed 50 year maximum rainfall.

COMPARISON OF THE STORM RAINFALL FOR KNOWN FLOOD PERIODS

In comparing the rainfall in various stations for known flood periods, nine stations were selected from those having the longest rainfall records. Four of these stations represent valley or foothill conditions, and five are mountain stations. The periods of known floods for which some rainfall records are available include eight storms in addition to the storm of March 2nd. . . . While the times during the day at which the day's readings are made will vary between stations, each station is presumably consistent in its own readings. . . .

Computing the storm rainfall values for each station in terms of the March 2nd record and obtaining the average percentage for each storm, the figures . . . seem to show that for the maximum day's rainfall, the March 2nd storm was the greatest, followed by the New Year's storm at 80 per cent and the 1921 storm at 78 per cent. For the total storm rainfall, the recent storm was the greatest, followed by the 1921 storm at 95 per cent and then by the 1914 storm at 79 per cent. The storms of 1884 and 1889 apparently show relatively low percentage values, but this may be explained by the absence of any mountain rainfall records. . . .

MAJOR STREAM CHANNELS—COMPARISON OF FLOODS

On the Los Angeles River, it is apparent that the recent flood materially exceeded any previous flood for which runoff records are available. It was from two to four times as large as the storm of New Year's, 1934, and about twice as big as any recorded flood previous.

· · ·

An early report on the concrete lining of the Los Angeles riverbed by the U.S. Army Corps of Engineers celebrated the use of such technology for "literally rebuilding" the river. The author describes it as a novel engineering approach that combines flood control and water conservation in the same project.

From Andrew R. Boone, "River Rebuilt to Curb Floods" (*Scientific American* 161 [November 1939]: 264–265. [Reproduced with permission. Copyright © 2016. Scientific American, a division of Nature America, Inc. All rights reserved.]).

"RIVER REBUILT TO CURB FLOODS

ENGINEERS ARE PROTECTING LOS ANGELES AND SURROUNDING AREA . . .

FLOOD CONTROL AND WATER CONSERVATION DUAL AIM"

Under conditions existing until recently, according to Major Theodore Wyman, Jr., U.S. Engineer Department district engineer, a great flood would practically cut off access to the city of Los Angeles, with its population of 1,500,000. In fact, Major Wyman pointed out that the wide plain on which Los Angeles is situated is under a more dangerous flood menace than any similar region in the United States.

Accordingly, Army engineers and the Los Angeles County Flood Control District are literally rebuilding the Los Angeles River, a stream which, in 40 miles, experiences a fall equal to that of the Mississippi River between Omaha, Nebraska, and the Gulf of Mexico. Rebuilding the river is part of a broader flood control plan. Already Los Angeles County has spent $60,000,000 in building parts of the protective works. Present plans call for an expenditure of $70,000,000 more. But amounts of money to be spent give no idea of the engineering difficulties and problems involved; not only must flood waters and debris of the discharging flood be curbed, but also as much water as possible must be conserved to replenish ground water storage. The life of much of southern California depends upon such stored waters.

FIGURE 36. The Los Angeles River being prepared for concrete.
Courtesy of the Los Angeles Public Library Photo Collection.

Work to date, recommended by the Board of Engineers, for Rivers and Harbors and approved by the Chief of Engineers, has been done at points where floor danger was most imminent. In foothill areas, some 600 basins and dams have been constructed to control the water flowing from these basins. Below the foothills and on the coastal plain, various channels have been enlarged, straightened, and provided with bank protection, or enclosed within reinforced concrete channels. . . .

Most important of the streams, insofar as their rampages may affect concentrated population, is the Los Angeles River. This stream, 70 miles in length, may be bone dry in summer, and then carry water at the rate of 90,000 cubic feet a second through downtown Los Angeles during a winter flood. Hence, to save congested areas within the city proper, as well as outlying areas, the improvements proposed for the river include construction of a leveed channel from its headwaters to the ocean; construction of three flood-control basins; and channel improvement in two washes which empty into the river, as well as on other tributaries. . . .

From many points of view, re-building this fractious stream presents engineering novelty. It is only part of a larger program, however: that of saving both life and property over a wide area of southern California and conserving water that agriculture and industry may not suffer. How well the engineers have built only time and flood can tell.

· · ·

Concreting riverbeds was a method not supported by all. Opponents argued that attacking the problem of flooding and mudslides in the foothills, where it began, would prevent inundation of the lowlands and not require concrete. The engineers and public officials who criticized the concrete solution remained in the minority as the concrete was poured. In this plea to the federal government, the representative of the Los Angeles chapter of a national civic organization argues that the concrete method for flood control is a massive waste of federal funds for the benefit of concrete and equipment manufacturers. In addition, it ignores the initial plans of flood control engineers to build less costly infrastructure in the mountains and foothills to prevent mudslides and flooding farther downstream.

From a copy of Anthony Pratt (Municipal League of Los Angeles) to [U.S.] Board of Engineers for Rivers and Harbors (December 11, 1939, Box 10, John Anson Ford Papers, Huntington Library, San Marino, CA).

Board of Engineers for Rivers & Harbours,
Washington, D.C.

Gentlemen:

The Municipal League of Los Angeles is an organization that for 39 years has been a watch dog on Municipal, County and School Board waste. It has especially exposed waste in alleged flood control programs that have been put over on the people by the big material manufacturing interests hereabout.

When after fighting for years, sometimes successfully, the graft in Flood Control projects under County Government administration, the problems were more recently dumped into the lap of the Federal Government, we looked on askance but hoped for the best in spite of the reputation for extravagance that has followed in the wake of many of the United States Army Engineers' reclamation and flood control projects. We still had the idea that though extravagant, these army engineers did do a good job.

So we have been quiescent while the recent millions of dollars have been spent here under their plans and with their sanctions.

But we can be quiescent no longer in view of the way their work in the Los Angeles County Flood Control District has signally failed in part and in view of the new report and recommendations of these engineers who are now advocating the expenditure of some $200,000,000 more along the same general lines that have been followed by them for the expenditure of the last $70,000,000 federal allotment to this Flood Control District.

The Municipal League has long strongly protested the twisting of the original program favored by four of the five engineers who reported for the county of Los Angeles in 1917 into a material man's paradise with one dam in San Gabriel Canyon that was to have been "the highest dam in the world," and that would require millions of dollars for cement alone.

The majority report of that original Flood Control Commission stressed the greater importance of keeping the rains, as they descended upon the mountains, up in the same mountain areas in the natural reservoirs beneath the soil, and in preventing erosion by such simple things as contour trenches, terraces and the humble check dam.

But the recommendations of the majority report were not followed. The first bond issue was thus diverted as to the modus operandi from its original purpose. It was for only $4,500,000 and the public was led to believe that the proper treatment for the higher altitudes could be effected by this original investment. But the material manufacturers and the big dam contractors proved too strong for our weak Board of Supervisors and after this first bond issue was spent according to the plans of the minority member of the Commission, Mr. Reagan, a second bond issue was proposed for $35,000,000, $25,000,000 of which was for the above mentioned "highest dam in the world," in connection with which one supervisor was convicted of taking an $80,000 bribe. The Municipal League opposed this bond issue but it was voted by politically spreading the promised benefits widely throughout the county.

The Executive Board of the Municipal League is now protesting to your Honorable Board of Engineers at Washington against these further flood control plans that contemplate another $200,000,000 largely for channel work in the valleys and that pay so little attention comparatively to the correct treatment in the mountain areas.

We trust that our protest may be thoroughly considered by you. John Anson Ford, the outstanding liberal supervisor of Los Angeles County and member of the Los Angeles County Flood Control Board, presented to our public forum last Tuesday an alternate suggestion that instead of the $200,000,000 as proposed $100,000,000 or as much thereof as may be necessary be used in the higher altitudes for creating, everywhere possible, small reservoirs and for small dams, check dams, terraces, contour trenches, etc.

We are sending copies of this letter expressing the sentiments of the Executive Board of the Municipal League to all the congressmen from this area and also to our Senator.

Yours very truly,
MUNICIPAL LEAGUE OF LOS ANGELES
By Anthony Pratt (Signed)
Secretary

. . .

In the 1920s, residents of Owens Valley complained that they had been cheated by Los Angeles water officials who had purchased their property and water rights. In a letter to Mary Austin, a portion of which is reproduced here, Bishop merchant Julian E. Eibeshutz states that the farmers did well in the transactions, but that the valley's business owners paid the price when the population decreased. At the same time he notes his belief that the valley is gradually turning from a robust agricultural region into a desert.

From Julian E. Eibeshutz to Mary Austin (May 8, 1925, AU2290, Mary Austin Papers, Huntington Library, San Marino, CA).

The City of Los Angeles has purchased nearly every acre of Ground from Georges Creek to Bishop—buying the water rights and conveying the water through an aqueduct across Mojave Desert to Los Angeles—I have a vision of our beautiful Ranch properties going back to Desert and our beautiful valley ruined—Our Towns are without any visible means of support—with the exception of Tourist Trade which is good for only about four months of the year and the principles and problems that we have fought out for years to bring this valley into a state of civilization wherein it would be a pleasure to dwell was all for nothing and we have been visited with a blight—

The Ranchers who sold are comfortably fixed as the city paid them good prices—You will probably remember the "old Fort" Country—Gormans, Walters, Shabbell, Densmores, Bells, etc.—They can all retire—some have moved from here[,] others will remain for a while—I do not know what the city intends doing with our communities but it looks as if we would be compelled to sue for reparations.

・ ・ ・

The acquisition of water for a thirsty Los Angeles forever left its mark in the Owens Valley. As described in this report by a committee in the California State Legislature, printed in 1931, the removal of water through the aqueduct left the Owens Lake and its drainage area utterly transformed. A prosperous agricultural and business environment in the valley became a desert, the lake a "shifting body of alkali, soda, sand and dust." Over the years, Los Angeles officials have carried on a variety of programs to mitigate the changes, often by court order, although contention between the city and Inyo County interests and environmentalists continues to this day.

From California Legislature, Senate, Special Investigating Committee on Water Situation in Inyo and Mono Counties, *Report of Special Investigating Committee on Water Situation in Inyo and Mono Counties* (Sacramento: California State Printing Office, 1931).

FINDINGS

The situation existing in the Owens River Valley, Inyo County, is very different from that of the Mono Basin in Mono County, and, therefore, we deal with these two situations separately.

The Owens River Valley is situated east and almost in the shadow of the lofty Sierra Nevada mountains. The snows from these mountains furnish an abundant supply of clear, pure mountain water, which reaches the valley through various creeks[,] and make up the supply for Owens River. This water formerly found its way into Owens Lake, which, at one time, was a large body of water in the southern end of the valley.

FIGURE 37. Dry Owens Lake and blowing alkali dust, 2008.
Courtesy of Eeekster (photographer Richard Ellis) via Wikimedia Commons.

The soil of this valley is exceedingly fertile, when irrigated, and raises valuable crops of alfalfa, grain, fruits and vegetables, and it furnishes abundant pasturage for cattle, and has been cultivated since 1860, continuously. The land, without water, will become barren and worthless and revert to sand and sagebrush, its former state.

The evidence shows that about the year 1860, the settlers moved into this valley, endured the dangers and privations attendant to pioneer life, improving the land, taking the water from the high Sierra for irrigation. Soon Owens Valley blossomed forth as one of the richest agricultural sections of the state of California. Several hundred farms and farm houses dotted its green meadows.

Thousands of head of cattle grazed in its fields. Valuable crops of hay and grain were produced, and hundreds of acres were planted to productive orchards of peaches, pears, apples and other deciduous fruits. The climatic condition, the fertile land and the natural beauty of the scenery made of this valley a veritable paradise.

Towns sprang up in the valley, supported and sustained by the rich farming areas. Bishop became the principal business center, and had, at one time, a population of approximately 2500. Independence, the county seat, Big Pine, Lone Pine and Laws were flourishing communities, and, in addition to these, were other smaller trade centers. All these communities were surrounded by rich agricultural lands that produced a large revenue. Testimony shows that up to the year 1923 each one of these towns did an enormous business with the agricultural elements.

These towns grew and flourished because of the agricultural development of the valley, and this development was made possible by the ample supply of water from the mountains on the west side of the valley. Substantial business houses of a permanent character were erected in these towns. Beautiful residences, comparable to those in other towns of California were built and occupied. Business flourished. Public buildings that would be a credit to any town or to any county were erected in the various communities; in short, Owens Valley became one of the most prosperous and beautiful agricultural sections of the State of California.

Testimony shows that in about the year 1904, the growing city of Los Angeles, realizing that the future prosperity of that city depended upon an abundant supply of pure water for domestic, industrial and municipal uses, began the task of building of the vast aqueduct a distance of nearly three hundred miles, to carry these waters to the city of Los Angeles. Prior to the construction of the aqueduct, the city of Los Angeles sent its agents into Owens Valley and began purchasing lands in order to secure the water rights appurtenant to these lands. This process continued until, at the present time, the city of Los Angeles owns about 90 per cent of the lands in the valley. The city of Los Angeles buys the lands for the water only, and the water is taken into the aqueduct. The rich lands formerly irrigated by this water are dried up and allowed to return to desert conditions. Orchards are torn up, buildings are torn down or burned, and, in a short time, lands that were rich and productive have returned to their former condition.

In addition to taking the surface water, the city of Los Angeles has put down a series of wells in the valley, approximately 150 in number. These wells are pumping constantly, and the water from them augments the supply of the aqueduct. In this manner, the underground water table of the valley has been lowered to the point where Owens Valley is drying up. Owens Lake is already dry, and what was once the lake bed is now a shifting body of alkali, soda, sand and dust.

The damage wrought by the taking of these waters is apparent. The farming lands purchased by the city of Los Angeles are reverting to desert. The lands not yet purchased are suffering from the shortage of water due to the exhaustion of the subsurface water by the pumping and drainage carried on by the city of Los Angeles. The former occupants of these lands have migrated to other portions of the State and the west. The few remaining landowners find themselves confronted with a condition of isolation. Their neighbors are gone. Their local markets are gone, and most of their ranches are being surrounded by complete desolation.

The remaining landowners now realize that they can not hold their lands and farms, and that they can not prosper without cooperative neighbors.

Damage to business houses and property in the towns that were supported or were dependent upon the farm areas is very apparent. These towns are dwindling away. With the farming lands which caused the towns to prosper gone, the towns are gradually dying. Business is lost. Residences must be abandoned. Most of these people must leave everything they have and go elsewhere to earn a livelihood. The water which sustained and gave life to the valley has been and is being taken out of the valley.

Your committee also found a condition existing as to the town of Keeler entirely different from that of the other part of the valley. Keeler is situated on the eastern edge of what was formerly Owens Lake. The lake now being dry, a vast body of alkali, soda and sand is whirled about by the valley winds and into the former prosperous town of Keeler, clouding the air and filling the roads and streets with sands not unlike drifted snow. Dust and dirt sift through the crevices in doors and windows and cover floors and furniture, making life at Keeler practically unbearable. The body of water formerly in Owens Lake moderated the temperature, but, as it is now dry, the summer heat is almost intolerable.

. . .

Harnessing the power of nature for the public good was a common progressive objective in the early twentieth century, although there would be many complaints later on. In this 1926 article in *Scientific American,* the title "The Subjugation of the Colorado" tells it all. Nature was there to be conquered, tamed, controlled, and used for the good of humankind.

From Guy Elliott Mitchell, "The Subjugation of the Colorado: Substituting Power, Light and Fertile Lands for Disastrous Flood Waters" (*Scientific American* 134 [March 1926]: 158–159. [Reproduced with permission. Copyright © 2016. Scientific American, a division of Nature America, Inc. All rights reserved.]).

"THE SUBJUGATION OF THE COLORADO

SUBSTITUTING POWER, LIGHT AND FERTILE LANDS FOR DISASTROUS FLOOD WATERS"

The great Colorado River of the west is no longer a mystery, an unknown danger. It has given up all of its secrets to engineering and scientific exploration and, even now, definite plans have been formulated to prevent its disastrous floods, to harness its vast power and to spread its huge volume of fertilizing, irrigating waters over millions of desert acres. The complete subjugation of the Colorado is an engineering undertaking of stupendous magnitude—one, not of millions but of hundreds of millions of dollars of cost.

THE MONSTER WILL BE TAMED

The Colorado has its sources in the high mountains of the Continental Divide. Its waters drop some 14,000 feet in their 1,500-mile course to the sea. Every workable horsepower in that great fall is to be utilized as needed—and, after this energy has been harnessed, the same waters, gathered from a watershed of 244,000 square miles, will be let out to irrigate millions of acres of thirsty, desert lands and there to produce crops of fabulous magnitude.

If there is poetry in engineering, surely the Colorado is a fascinating theme for contemplation. A wild and cruel monster, a giant of destruction to human life and property, its evil tendencies may all be corrected; it may bring staple foods and luscious fruits to millions of people; it may turn the wheels of a thousand industries; and though now a region of almost utter inaccessibility, a fact not very generally realized, it may become a place of lake and canyon splendor surpassing perhaps anything in the world to be visited with ease and comfort.

Looking somewhat ahead of the present interest in the Colorado, the United States Geological Survey has for many years been making a close study of the river and its great watershed. The Survey's hydraulic and topographic engineers have traversed and mapped every foot of its great canyon and its many tributary canyons, and its geologists have examined the rock structure of its multitude of dam and reservoir sites; for the river can be controlled and utilized only by the creation of great artificial lakes or flood-storage reservoirs. We are apt to think of storage reservoirs as ponds of a score or possibly a hundred acres or so in extent, retained by masonry walls; but the storage lakes of the Colorado will be hundreds of square miles in extent and they will be bounded by rugged canyon walls.

The volume of the flow of the Colorado and that of its tributaries has been measured and plotted by the Geological Survey engineers during a period of over twenty years. This close scrutiny of the behavior of the river, of its range in flow from a comparative trickle of 3,000 cubic feet of water per second to wild floods of over 200,000 second-feet, and the examination of inaccessible dam sites, culminated two years ago in the voyage by engineers and geologists through the 200 most dangerous miles of the Grand Canyon itself.

And now comes the result of this labor of magnitude, analyzed and presented in a government engineering report—a definite plan for the complete subjugation and utilization of the river. It is a project to construct 13 great dams and reservoirs and create hundreds of miles of artificial lakes, whereby all the floods of the Colorado will become only historic; since they will be converted into a great resource by the utilization of all the water for power and irrigation.

ONE COMPREHENSIVE PLAN ESSENTIAL

E. C. La Rue, the author of the Colorado River report and plan, is a hydraulic engineer of the Geological Survey, and throughout the southwest you may often hear him referred to as the "father of the Colorado." He has known the river for half a lifetime; he has made hundreds of miles of boat trips through its wild and treacherous canyon reaches charged with the responsibility of selecting all possible dam sites and supervising their survey.

But even in this report, the Geological Survey is not presuming to promote any particular power or irrigation project. It is making available the mass of information needed for outlining a feasible scheme for the full development of the river and especially for an orderly and wise planning. The river must be developed as a single undertaking, piecemeal it is true, but according to a general plan; and no single or initial project must be permitted which will ruin or detract from the later and greater possible ultimate development. In order that this may be accomplished, there must be government regulation of the engineering phases of the work.

The beginning in construction will doubtless be to prevent flood damage. There is urgent need for the building of a dam to protect the hundred or more million dollars invested along the lower reaches of the river in the Imperial Valley and elsewhere. The recurrence of any one of the big floods of the Colorado would wipe out this property and perhaps cause great loss of life—and it may come next year, or in any year. It is also probable that a dam for the development of power will be built at an early date. But these or any other dams should be built as part of the whole, big adventure.

· · ·

In a 1928 article, Elwood Mead, commissioner of the U.S. Bureau of Reclamation, referred to the project as "Conquering the Colorado." As was common at the time, environmental consequences of such an undertaking were not considered, in light of the "interest that is worldwide."

From Elwood Mead, "Conquering the Colorado" (*Literary Digest* 97 [April 21, 1928]: 50–58).

"CONQUERING THE COLORADO

BOULDER DAM—SYMBOL OF THE EPIC CONQUEST OF THE SOUTHWEST"

Into the hottest and driest part of the country the Colorado River brings the melted snows of the loftiest summits of the main range of the Rockies.

It carries the clear, cold water of the Green River morainal lakes into a region of lonesome brown deserts and to homes which under irrigation are made beautiful by a tropical opulence of fruit and foliage.

This water, symbol of motion, life, and change, is the key to the future of the Southwest. It is needed to develop mineral riches of southern Nevada, to irrigate the fertile unpeopled mesa lands of western Arizona, and to give to cities like Los Angeles and San Diego in California the water essential to their growth.

Without regulation and control, the river has comparatively little value. When the snows are melting it is turbulent and destructive; when they are gone it shrinks to a shadow of what it was a few months before. In its highest stages it carries water enough to irrigate a million acres of land in a single day; at its lowest recorded flow it will do little more than wet the bottoms of canals already built. Although the limits of profitable development of the unregulated river have been reached, if its floods are stored and released to meet the needs of agriculture, to light cities and turn the wheels of factories, it will feed and clothe ten million more people than now live there.

When President Coolidge signed the Boulder Dam bill on the 21st of last December, he ended an epic struggle in Congress which had lasted eight years. It had taken Congress that long to decide how the Colorado should be regulated and who should do it. He also began a new era in the reclamation of the arid West and the harnessing of its rivers for that service.

The prolonged discussions in Congress, and the months given to hearings by committees, were due largely to the fact that this bill embodied about every problem of reclamation[,] and its discussion started an evolution of ideas and methods that is still going on.

The pioneer idea of development was for each man to look out for himself and let the devil take the hindmost. Individuals and companies claimed rivers, and dug canals to divert them, without thinking what others were doing above or below on the same stream. We have reached the end of that kind of unrelated action. It has already brought contests in the courts between states, and bitterness of feeling between communities. Boulder Dam and its great related works are to be built by the federal government under a water-right compact framed by representatives of the seven states of the river's watershed and ratified by the legislatures of six of those states. It has enlisted the cooperation of the nation, states, cities, irrigation districts, and important hydroelectric corporations.

To harness this river requires a dam 700 feet high, nearly twice the height of any now in existence. Above this dam will be a lake 100 miles long and nearly 600 feet deep. The lake will have a surface area of 140,000 acres and will hold 26,000,000 acre-feet of water, enough to cover the state of Kentucky one foot deep. It will not only be the largest artificial reservoir in this country but it will have ten times the capacity of the Elephant Butte reservoir, which is now the largest. The power plant will generate 1,000,000 horsepower, equal to all those of Niagara. The All-American Canal, which will be 200 feet wide on the bottom and 20 feet deep, will carry water enough to irrigate nearly one hundred thousand acres in a single day. The mere statement of these dimensions grips the imagination. It has aroused an interest that is worldwide.

· · ·

The quality of Colorado River water for public consumption was an issue raised by several critics who believed it could never be made pure enough to drink. One such critic was Los Angeles businessman Lewis Clark Stubbins. He included such an argument in a much longer speech he delivered during the 1931 political campaign before the vote on whether to support the bond measure to finance the Colorado Aqueduct project. For Stubbins, water quality was but one reason of many that should have convinced voters to oppose the bonds.

It turns out that he was right to a certain degree. Salinity of Colorado River water increased over the years because of agricultural practices and the decrease of the water flow for other uses. Agricultural land in the lower area suffered tremendous damage, which resulted in massive costs to mitigate.

From Lewis Clark Stubbins, "Vote No on September 29th, 1931, on the Colorado Aqueduct Bonds" (pamphlet, 1931, 4–6, held by Special Collections, Claremont Colleges Library, Claremont, CA).

1. Quality of Water.

No matter what may be your conclusion regarding the other points, the quality of water is paramount. If it is not fit to use after obtained, all other considerations are of no moment.

A tremendous technical controversy over this question has raged ever since the Colorado scheme has been proposed.

Study of the quality by the United States Geological Survey and the Reclamation Service as well as many technical experts from various Colleges and Universities have been made and the resultant conflicting conclusions published.

Out of all this great mass of conflicting statements and opinions a few facts stand out. We all know Colorado Water when clarified is used for Domestic purposes in Needles, Yuma, and Imperial Valley. Against this statement I will call your attention to an article in one of the Metropolitan Dailies of August 11th, which carried an article regarding labor conditions at Hoover Dam, from which the following sentence is quoted:

> "Discarding the River water on account of its danger to health at this time of the year, the contractors are hauling water from Las Vegas Artesian Springs to the Dam Area and this is distributed in milk cans."

Extensive salt beds exist on the Virgin River, which will be flooded by Hoover Dam. The Metropolitan Water District in its report entitled "Summary of Surveys, etc.", published in December, 1930, on page 18, states, "Recent topographical surveys by the Metropolitan Water District show the area of salt actually exposed to solution to be but 1.8 acres with 4.6 acres of soil containing more or less salt."

I personally have spent days walking over thousands of acres of salt impregnated lands where veritable mountains of salt exist, all of which will be flooded by the Reservoir.

Charles R. Fletcher, formerly Geologist for the Union Pacific Railway Company, after describing the deposit and referring to its vast extent and great though unknown depth said, "I have protested for years that if the salt deposits in the vicinity of the confluence of the Colorado and Virgin Rivers be inundated, as it will by the Black Canyon Reservoir, its water WILL BE UNFIT FOR DOMESTIC, AGRICULTURAL AND MUNICIPAL USES."

Analysis of Colorado water indicates salts in solution under present conditions are near the point of maximum tolerance. Flooding these vast salt beds cannot do other than increase to some degree the salt content; and evaporation from the Hoover Reservoir will further concentrate this salt.

I am not prepared to state, although a good many do, that after the construction of Hoover Dam, Colorado River water will be unfit for human consumption, but I do fearlessly say that after delivered to Southern California it will provide Los Angeles with, by long odds, the poorest Municipal supply of any large City in the Country.

· · ·

As part of the Los Angeles River and Owens Valley Aqueduct projects, reservoirs were built to store water for later use. In the case of the Boulder Dam project on

FIGURE 38. Lake Mead in 2010 showing its white "bathtub ring" illustrating the drop in the water level over the years.
Courtesy of Tom Sitton, photographer.

the Colorado River, "conquering nature" included the creation of what was, at the time, the world's largest human-made lake. In this 1938 article in *Scientific American,* the new lake is described as being filled for the purpose of water storage. Since then, Lake Mead has also been used for all manner of recreational purposes, although its level has dropped considerably in the last few decades.

From "Lake Mead, Largest Man-Made" (*Scientific American* 158 [February 1938]: 108–109. [Reproduced with permission. Copyright © 2016. Scientific American, a division of Nature America, Inc. All rights reserved.]).

"LAKE MEAD, LARGEST MAN-MADE"

In the desert of the southwest, a new and major lake is forming, Lake Mead, created by Boulder Dam. Named for the late Dr. Elwood Mead, Commissioner of Reclamation during the period of construction of Boulder Dam in Black Canyon of the Colorado River, Lake Mead is by far the largest man-made body of water in the world.

It extends up the Colorado River 101 miles at this time (autumn, 1937) and eventually will reach a maximum length of 111 miles. It will be eight miles wide at the widest point and, when filled, will have a maximum depth at the dam of 589 feet.

Lake Mead will store 30,500,000 acre-feet of water, sufficient when expressed in terms of gallons to supply 5000 gallons for each and every person on earth. Today it is slightly more than half filled. It now has a depth of about 460 feet and covers more than 91,000 acres.

Prior to 1935, there were few localities in the world more forbidding or more difficult to access than the bed of what now is Lake Mead. In the midst of a desert and desert mountains, the Colorado River then flowed through this area principally at the bottom of tremendous canyons. Only a few parties of daring explorers had ever traversed the length of the future Lake Mead, and many of the side or branch canyons, now covered in the lake, were unexplored.

When the diversion channels were closed at Boulder Dam February 1, 1935, Lake Mead immediately began to form. One year later, it held 3,000,000 acre-feet of water. Two years later, it contained 9,000,000 and was extending far up the river, through the sheer-walled Boulder Canyon, through Virgin, Iceberg, and Travertine canyons and was beginning to reach into the lower and unvisited end of the Grand Canyon itself. It can safely be navigated now over this entire reach of river.

The Colorado River was a fluctuating stream. It still is variable above Lake Mead, although Boulder Dam has made it a reliable, perennial watercourse downstream. When the snows of the mountains at its headwater melt in the spring, great floods move down the Colorado. After they have passed, the flow drops erratically to little more than a creek. The floods do not pass Boulder Dam, but are caught and stored to fill in the valleys of the flow in the summer and fall to protect the water users downstream.

As a result of these periodic floods, Lake Mead grows by fits and starts. It rises rapidly from March to July, but will decrease in size between August and February. During three or four months, the inflow into Lake Mead is greatly in excess of the outflow through Boulder Dam. But during the remainder of the year, the inflow and outflow are about equal or the outflow exceeds the inflow.

During 1936, 5,634,425 acre-feet of water were allowed to pass Boulder Dam. In the future and until the states of the upper Colorado River basin are prepared to use the water allotted to them, this diversion may increase to the normal flow of the river, or about 15,000,000 acre-feet a year. The amount of water diverted through the dam, of course, has a definite bearing on the speed with which Lake Mead fills. Another factor is the total amount of run-off in the river above the dam. This varies with the rain and snowfall over the watershed. If normal conditions prevail, Lake Mead may be filled in three years.

· · ·

Earthquakes! Always a heavy jolt to the natural landscape, they were not antici-pated in the original planning of the Boulder (later Hoover) Dam project, since the area was not known as earthquake country. But many earthquakes shook the area as Lake Mead filled and long after. Two measuring 5.0 on the Richter scale rocked the area in 1937, and hundreds more occurred until the 1960s, when the completion of the Glen Canyon Dam helped to moderate the flow of water down-river and reduced the occurrences of quakes. But the shakers haven't stopped, as evidenced by notable quakes in the area in 2014 and 2015.

From "Quakes Linked to Lake Mead" (*Los Angeles Times,* May 19, 1939. [Used with permission of The Associated Press. Copyright © 2015. All rights reserved.]).

"QUAKES LINKED TO LAKE MEAD

COLORADO WATER BEHIND HOOVER DAM SUSPECTED OF CAUSING SHOCKS"

Washington, May 18 (AP)—Waters of the Colorado River which have backed up behind Hoover Dam to form Lake Mead were linked today to a sharp increase in earthquakes.

Admiral L. O. Colbert, director of the Coast and Geodetic Survey, disclosed dur-ing House hearings on appropriations for the Commerce Department that there were no records of earthquakes in the area in the 10 years prior to the filling of the lake.

Water began to back up in the lake in 1935, he said, and 65 quakes were felt in the vicinity in 1936 and 1937. A seismograph was installed in 1938, and during that year it recorded 505 earthquakes, of which 55 were strong enough to be felt by persons living near the lake.

"Three of these were very strong," the admiral added.

He said the Budget Bureau is considering a proposal for the Coast and Geodetic Survey to spend $25,000 studying the situation.

Epilogue

What's Next? What's the Future?

Given our ambition for this book—that it will carry you through documents and ideas back to a river and urban past that must be grappled with in order to fully understand the present—we would be remiss if we did not at least contemplate the future of metropolitan Los Angeles in terms of exactly those riparian places and spaces. The future, unknown and unknowable, is nonetheless inextricably tied to what has come before—which roads or paths were taken or not and how the history of rivers moves and shifts and changes course like a river itself.

Los Angeles celebrated, in 2013, the hundredth anniversary of the opening of the Los Angeles Aqueduct. It was an anniversary that prompted a wide variety of responses—from celebration to antipathy and everything in between. For many, the century's mark passed without notice or care. For some, the moment offered an opportunity to celebrate all that metropolitan Los Angeles had become since 1913, watered in part (in large part) by the snowmelt waters of the Owens River. For others, however, the centennial offered the chance to look again at the "water grab" performed a hundred years earlier. The anniversary meant that Los Angeles, or its municipal Department of Water and Power, was yet again trying to wrap a bold and ultimately imperial play and ploy in adjectives that speak to legacy, growth, inevitability, vision, and ambition.

To be sure, the hundred-year history of the Los Angeles Aqueduct is fraught and deeply complicated. Nothing is simple about moving a river hundreds of miles from its bed. It wasn't simple in 1913, and it is certainly not simple today; and we could say that the matter grows more complex with each passing year. For one thing, there are two aqueducts now, two giant metal straws of cavernous diameter sucking on the melted Sierra snowpack and hustling it southwest to a thirsty global metropolis. Atop all the engineering and physics and hydrology issues at stake—and they are legion—there remain issues of upkeep and maintenance and environmental impact.

That is but the tip of an aqueduct iceberg. Long-simmering resentment and anger in the Owens Valley (especially vociferous there, for obvious reasons, but not only there) about the creation of the Los Angeles Aqueduct has, as we might have expected, found its way into courtrooms and litigation. Remarkable legal decisions have resulted, in more than one instance, that have altered the perceived, if misleading, simplicity of two big straws stuck into a flowing river. Citing history (as in the case of a once-full, now-dry Owens Lake) and health concerns tying dust to pulmonary and respiratory disease and difficulty, antagonistic individuals and organizations took on the city of Los Angeles and its chief water agency and won a series of important battles and concessions. These amount essentially to Los Angeles leaving water in the Owens Valley or putting some of it back. The city is now responsible for a series of mitigation exercises that is putting water back into the ancient lakebed of Owens Lake, as well as into Mono Lake as a protective measure for the fragile geologic structures within it. Legal action is not likely to abate in the short term, and it is entirely possible that climate-change ramifications (most specifically the depleted Sierra Nevada snowpack) will add to the complexities of mitigation and further legal disputes between entities in the Owens Valley, or their proxies, and the city of Los Angeles.

Climate change is undoubtedly going to play a huge role in determining the future of the Metropolitan Water District's place in supplying water from the Colorado River to its client entities, with the Los Angeles Department of Water and Power being chief among them. As the water district's ability to draw from the state water project (a largely north-south conduit bringing water to Southern California) evaporates—its allotment has gone down dramatically in recent years— the role of the Colorado River becomes even more prominent. The legal issues attendant on this situation are, if anything, more complex than those in dispute regarding the Owens River, the Owens Valley, and the thirsty giant metropolis far to the southwest.

So, too, is the fate and future of the Colorado River a complex, tangled tale of water, climate change, international treaties, and widespread thirst. Asked to water great chunks of seven states, as well as parts of northern Mexico, the Colorado River watershed is the most important in the United States, perhaps even in North America. Recent onslaughts of drought across the American West have resulted in drastic changes in the ways in which Colorado River water is stored and delivered to a divergent and far-flung customer base of agencies, municipalities, and entire states and nations. By virtue of long-standing agreements, Southern California is entitled to a lion's share of the Colorado River (always dependent on the annual wintertime Rocky Mountain snowpack on the western slope of the Continental

Divide). This legal allotment amounts to over four million acre-feet of water (an acre-foot is a standard water measurement: one acre spread with water to a depth of one foot, or three hundred thousand gallons of water). Because the state-to-state agreements were formulated in especially "wet" years, and because California threw its considerable weight around back in the early 1920s, when the most important agreements were signed, the Golden State can keep drawing water while states such as Arizona and Nevada will lose water . . . all from a water source that is itself losing water to climate change at a fast (and accelerating) rate.

As drought and climate change alter the snowpack levels from year to year in the Colorado high country, the cities, states, and water agencies will continue to struggle with the consequences. And these consequences will of course affect individuals at every point along the Colorado River's watercourse. Preservation and conservation efforts will and must continue. These will take many forms, and undoubtedly new innovations will come to the fore. Water restrictions—how much, how often, aimed at what, and at what times—will become more common. Water reuse will rise in popularity—household water will find its way more and more often into outdoor and gardening use. Roofs will be better fit with water catchment devices for rainwater capture. Drain spouts will catch water instead of rushing it off to storm sewers and the ocean. Trees will be planted in places, such as school playgrounds, once covered in asphalt or concrete (trees catch water and hold it around their roots).

Broader innovations will have to be implemented as well. Individual efforts—which will include smartphone technology applied to, for example, household irrigation systems and timing (off it goes when it rains)—will make some difference. But bigger actions, on a statewide or even a federal scale, with regulatory or enforcement teeth, are needed. Water trading between states will rise in importance, and these innovations will have to be carefully modeled and regulated. Water pricing will be intricately related, of course, and it is likely that disparate water costs, which are now the rule rather than the exception, will be leveled out (though allowed to fluctuate in times of relative abundance or relative scarcity). Perhaps most important, the rural-urban divide regarding water use will need to be addressed and hard decisions made, backed up by legislative innovation. Rural users account for most of the water use—by far—across California and the entire American Southwest. Demand is rising in urban centers, but so much water is being used on agricultural crops that the urban demand—however modest by comparison—is not being efficiently met. What kinds of crops are grown, and how they are irrigated, will and must change, lest Southern California face even worse conditions born of water scarcity, drought, and the loose and inefficient "water culture" that has been allowed to develop over the past century.

Environmental awareness and environmental sustainability will go hand in hand with greater awareness of water's preciousness and scarcity. We think historical knowledge is required in order to gain that kind of critical perspective. One of the key features of changing cultural and environmental attitudes will be simple "river awareness" in California cities, which, at this writing, we can say is growing. Los Angeles is and will be the most important locale for this, and all attention will be focused on the rivers of the Los Angeles basin. Ironically, perhaps (given its puny size in relation to far bigger rivers and watersheds), none will be more important than the Los Angeles River.

The Los Angeles River is the riparian canary in the coal mine of Southern California sustainability. It has, in just over one hundred years, gone from promise to problem and now again to promise in the regional imagination. After 1941, postwar floods, spilling out across the basin, led to more concrete being poured into and up the banks of the river. Still a vital cog in the machine of flood control—the concrete that encases the body of the river is critical to corralling floodwaters—the Los Angeles River is simultaneously the central focus of a great deal of environmental reimagining of green space and greenbelts throughout the metropolitan Los Angeles basin. From biking paths to kayaking and possible reintroduction of steelhead trout, the river is being rethought in very large terms and scales as the twenty-first century opens; much of this is due to the long-standing advocacy and activism of groups, none more critical than the Friends of the Los Angeles River. "Greening" the Los Angeles River, pulling out *some* of the concrete straitjacket, and becoming more aware of the riparian environment at the very center of a global metropolis of millions of people, is a large-scale effort—of imagination, of money, and of engineering and environmental know-how. Each innovation, each step forward, will further the collective knowledge about rivers and about water, and this consciousness change (from "what Los Angeles River?" to "our Los Angeles River") can only lead to further benefits in conservation, preservation, and "waterwise" awareness. That path to a differently imagined riparian future will be complicated, with political, fiscal, and hydrological hurdles of daunting scale strewn hither and yon at each step of the way. We suggest optimism about the Los Angeles River, a faith born of diehard grassroots activism and a level of renewed political leadership gazing on a river too-long ignored or expected to provide but a single, flood-control purpose across the landscape it traverses. Perhaps now more than ever, the Los Angeles River is a site of dreams and disagreements, as various constituencies imagine what it *could* or *might* become; and as such futures are pondered, so, too, are questions about where the money comes from and who and how people (and nonhumans) benefit from riparian changes large and small.

This is not to say that the other two rivers are any less important. They are hugely important. But the symbolic burden placed on the Los Angeles River is, especially within the Los Angeles Basin, palpable and magnetic. "How are we doing?" people ask, wondering about water, water shortages, water conservation. And the answer, for many at least, will be found with reference to the Los Angeles River. However, to the north and east, the fate of the Owens River, and especially the Owens Valley, dry and getting drier, will provide additional perspective. And much of that will be colored by controversy: what can Los Angeles do, what should Los Angeles do, as environmental penance for its century-old role in desiccating a landscape? The questions can and will be asked regarding "how are we doing?" up there, up in the Owens Valley. That site, since midcentury, has prompted lawsuits against the city of Los Angeles for water loss and the resulting environmental damage. What can people—through advocacy and activism—claim or insist, and what can various courts or legal decisions obligate the city of Los Angeles to do? These are not issues that will go away, either; on the contrary, as dryness accelerates and snowpacks retreat, these issues will creep up in the headlines and in the lists of imperatives for the region and its populace. We simply urge that such awareness go hand in hand with appreciation of the interlocking histories and meanings of, for example, Los Angeles and the Owens River.

So, too, with the mighty Colorado. Entire careers are forged out of figuring out the dynamic realities of that river's place in the American West. Where does the river go? Who gets to decide? Which state or agency or nation gets to dip the largest buckets into it? And where to they get to dip? Where do the rights of states come into dialogue or conflict with the rights of indigenous people whose ancestral or reservation homelands sit alongside the river? How does Mexico interact with the various states that, in their thirst, deplete the Colorado so that it now peters out far from its former mouth on the Gulf of California?

Southern California lives because it can take so much Colorado River water to satisfy the thirst of its people and the thirst of what it grows. What happens if that gets shut off, or, more likely, what happens if the flow gets cut back, by law, by drought, by climate change? Major international decisions reached by treaty in the years since 1941 have reduced the amount of water Southern California can take from the Colorado River, in favor of other states, indigenous polities, or Mexico. One thing is sure: the Colorado River cannot supply all the water that treaties or other agreements promise, and this has been true for decades. It carries a great deal of water. But not enough to meet demand, unless that demand is cut by conservation or other water-saving practices. Furthermore, what happens if the region's reliance upon water from Northern California, by means of the state water project (a "fourth river," which we do not take up in this book), becomes ever more compromised by state decisions that cut off supplies going to Southern California through the Metropolitan Water District's systems? Less Colorado River water, less Northern California water—where will those roads take us?

Amid all the uncertainties of rivers and waters, one thing is incontrovertible: the Colorado, the Owens, the Los Angeles: these are not infinite bodies of flowing water. They wax and they wane, they dry up (in actuality, or relatively, in response to wetter periods or years). Legal decisions act as dams, shutting off water that used to go from "here" to "there."

The Colorado River System

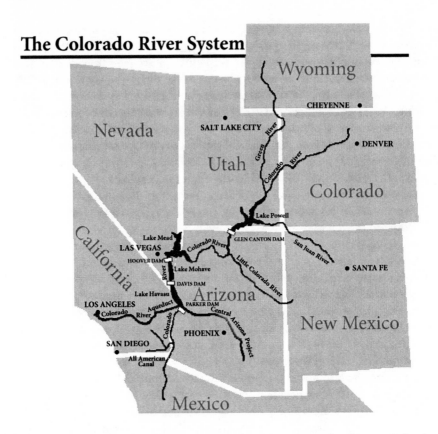

MAP 3. Besides providing water and hydroelectrical power to Los Angeles, the entire Colorado River system provides these resources to large areas of seven states, as well as northwestern Mexico. The gradual drainage of the river owing to drought, climate change, and other factors will continue to have a profound effect on a major portion of the American West.
Courtesy of the California Legislative Analyst's Office, Sacramento, California.

Arid times are here. Drought times are here. New rivers will not arise to solve the problems. We are stuck with what we have, and we want you to know what we have—what you have—and how we got from there to here, from then to now. This is a history we all share, just as it is a future we must all help to make better. One way to get there is to know more.

NOTES

PREFACE

1. William Deverell and Tom Sitton, eds., *California Progressivism Revisited* (Berkeley: University of California Press, 1994); Tom Sitton and William Deverell, eds., *Metropolis in the Making: Los Angeles in the 1920s* (Berkeley: University of California Press, 2001); Tom Sitton, *Grand Ventures: The Banning Family in the Shaping of Southern California* (San Marino, CA: Huntington Library Press, 2010).

INTRODUCTION

1. Although it is beyond the scope and attention of this book, the San Gabriel River, east of the city limits of Los Angeles, is also an important historical and contemporary riparian environment.

2. See, generally, Greg Hise and William Deverell, *Land of Sunshine: Toward an Environmental History of Metropolitan Los Angeles* (Berkeley: University of California Press, 2005) and, more specifically, John McPhee's reprinted essay in same.

CHAPTER 1. RIVERS OF GROWTH

The three chapter epigraphs are from the following sources, respectively: *Chinatown*, Paramount Pictures, 1974; Catherine Mulholland, *William Mulholland and the Rise of Los Angeles* (Berkeley: University of California Press, 2000), 128; *Los Angeles Times*, November 6, 1913.

1. See Mary Austin's letter in "Correspondence," *New Republic* 42 (April 8, 1925): 186. The letter could not be printed in this volume because of copyright restrictions.

CHAPTER 2. HARNESSING THE RIVERS

The two chapter epigraphs are from the following sources, respectively: Los Angeles County Coroner's Inquest, 1928, as cited in Norris Hundley Jr., *The Great Thirst: Californians and Water, 1770s–1990s* (Berkeley: University of California Press, 1992), 166; testimony from the Los Angeles County Coroner's Inquest, cited in Charles F. Outland, *Man-Made Disaster: The Story of St. Francis Dam* (Glendale, CA: A. H. Clark, 1963), 378.

CHAPTER 3. RIVERS IN NATURE

The chapter epigraph is from Los Angeles Board of Public Service Commissioners, *Complete Report on Construction of the Los Angeles Aqueduct* (Los Angeles Board of Public Service Commissioners, 1916), 9.

STUDY QUESTIONS FOR CONSIDERATION

GROWTH STUDY QUESTIONS

1. How do you think Los Angeles would have developed had the Los Angeles River not been channelized during the twentieth century? Can you compare the story of Los Angeles and its namesake river with those of other rivers in other cities at the same time or in other eras? How?
2. What is the current understanding of the role of the Los Angeles River in Greater Los Angeles? What are the differing points of view?
3. How would you describe the interconnectedness of the Colorado, Owens, and Los Angeles Rivers? Are there particular moments, years, or eras in which you think the histories of these three rivers overlap in significant ways? If so, when and why?
4. Can you find any evidence to suggest that ideas about water's scarcity or about water preservation played any role in the early twentieth-century history of any of the three rivers?

TECHNOLOGY STUDY QUESTIONS

1. Do you think there are differences in the technical skill used on, and the approach to the histories of, the three rivers under review here? Was the paving of the Los Angeles River a technologically more sophisticated operation than the transfer of the Owens River to the city limits of Los Angeles? Was the construction of Hoover Dam and the Colorado River Aqueduct the grandest of these acts of technological enterprise and riparian development? Defend your rankings with a few sentences explaining your point of view.

2. Big engineering projects such as those we have studied in this book are not limited to the Progressive Era. How would you compare—and with what measurements—something like the transcontinental railroad project of the Civil War era to the Colorado River damming and aqueduct projects a lifetime later?

3. How would you compare the relative importance of the generation of electricity by means of hydroelectric processes and of the provision of freshwater by the Colorado River system?

NATURE STUDY QUESTIONS

1. What do you think are the trade-offs in the use of concrete in the Los Angeles River, as far as environmental and safety issues are concerned? Why have ideas about the river undergone real shifts in the last generation or so?

2. Compare the watershed size and the river flow capacity of the three rivers in visual format (graph, drawing, etc.).

3. Over the past decade or so, how have rising aridity, decreasing snowpack, and hotter temperatures affected each of the three rivers and its role in supplying water to Southern California?

CHRONOLOGY

1825   Flood results in the Los Angeles River changing its course and emptying into San Pedro Bay instead of Ballona Creek.

1884   Major flood in Southern California.

1889   Major flood in Southern California.

1902   Los Angeles purchases its water system from a private company.

1905   Los Angeles voters approve $1.5 million in bonds to purchase land in Inyo County in order to transfer water from Owens River.

Colorado River breaks through into Imperial Valley and eventually forms Salton Sea.

1907   Los Angeles voters approve $23 million in bonds for construction of Owens River Aqueduct.

1912   Report of the Aqueduct Investigation Board criticizes construction and private investments.

1913   Owens Valley Aqueduct is completed, and water flows to Los Angeles.

1914   Major flooding in Southern California spurs flood control planning.

1915   Los Angeles County Flood Control District is formed.

1922   Colorado River Compact apportioning water to two groups of states is signed by representatives of seven states, in Santa Fe, New Mexico.

First Swing-Johnson Bill to build Boulder Dam and All-American Canal fails.

1923   Los Angeles City engineers begin survey of Colorado River for water aqueduct.

Six States (all but Arizona) ratify Colorado River Compact.

Second Swing-Johnson Bill to build Boulder Dam and All-American Canal fails.

1924   Colorado River Aqueduct Association organized in Pasadena.

First bombing of Owens River Aqueduct.

1925   First bill to approve creation of metropolitan water districts in California is introduced.

Los Angeles voters approve $2 million in bonds for Colorado River project.

1926   Third Swing-Johnson Bill fails in Congress.

1927   Metropolitan water district bill in California passes and is signed by governor.

1928   Metropolitan Water District of Southern California is incorporated.

Boulder Canyon Project Act (Swing-Johnson Bill) passes and is signed by President Calvin Coolidge.

St. Francis Dam fails; at least four hundred deaths result.

1930   Contracts specifying allocation of water signed by secretary of interior and Metropolitan Water District of Southern California.

Contracts specifying allocation of electrical power signed by secretary of interior and Metropolitan Water District of Southern California and by the latter's individual cities.

Los Angeles voters approve $38.8 million in bonds to extend the Owens River Aqueduct system to the Mono Basin.

1931   Contract for construction of Boulder Dam awarded to Six Companies, Inc.

Voters approve $220-million bond issue in cities of Metropolitan Water District of Southern California by a five-to-one margin.

Comprehensive Plan for Flood Control approved for Los Angeles County.

1933   Contract executed by the federal government and the Metropolitan Water District of Southern California for construction of Parker Dam.

1934   Contract for construction of Parker Dam awarded to Six Companies, Inc.

Major flooding in Los Angeles County; forty deaths in La Crescenta.

1935   U.S. Supreme Court enjoins Arizona governor from using state militia to stop construction of Parker Dam.

Congress approves Emergency Relief Act to address 1934 flooding nationwide.

1936   Boulder Dam is completed.

Flood Control Act authorizes $70 million for improvements and places U.S. Army Corps of Engineers in charge of major projects.

1938   Major flooding in Los Angeles results in almost fifty deaths in Los Angeles County.

1941   Colorado River Aqueduct water reaches cities of the Metropolitan Water District of Southern California.

Congress approves Los Angeles County flood control plan for major construction throughout the Los Angeles County system.

SELECTED BIBLIOGRAPHY

Bigger, Richard. *Flood Control in Metropolitan Los Angeles.* Berkeley: University of California Press, 1959.

Blomquist, William A. *Dividing the Waters: Governing Groundwater in Southern California.* San Francisco: ICS Press, 1992.

Cooper, Erwin. *Aqueduct Empire: A Guide to Water in California, Its Turbulent History and Its Management Today.* Glendale, CA: A. H. Clark, 1968.

Davis, Margaret Leslie. *Rivers in the Desert: William Mulholland and the Inventing of Los Angeles.* New York: HarperCollins, 1993.

Deverell, William. *Whitewashed Adobe: The Rise of Los Angeles and the Remaking of Its Mexican Past.* Berkeley: University of California Press, 2004.

Elkin, Sarah S. *How Local Politics Shape Federal Policy: Business, Power, and the Environment in Twentieth-Century Los Angeles.* Chapel Hill: University of North Carolina Press, 2011.

Erie, Steven P. *Beyond Chinatown: The Metropolitan Water District, Growth, and the Environment in Southern California.* Stanford, CA: Stanford University Press, 2006.

Fogelson, Robert M. *The Fragmented Metropolis: Los Angeles, 1850–1930.* Cambridge, MA: Harvard University Press, 1967.

Gottlieb, Robert, and Margaret FitzSimmons. *Thirst for Growth: Water Agencies as Hidden Government in California.* Tucson: University of Arizona Press, 1991.

Gumprecht, Blake. *The Los Angeles River: Its Life, Death, and Possible Rebirth.* Baltimore: Johns Hopkins University Press, 1999.

Hiltzik, Michael A. *Colossus: Hoover Dam and the Making of the American Century.* New York: Free Press, 2010.

Hoffman, Abraham. *Vision or Villainy: Origins of the Owens Valley–Los Angeles Water Controversy.* College Station: Texas A & M University Press, 1981.

Hundley, Norris, Jr. *The Great Thirst: Californians and Water, 1770s–1990s.* Berkeley: University of California Press, 1992.

———. *Water and the West: The Colorado River Compact and the Politics of Water in the American West.* Berkeley: University of California Press, 1975.

Hundley, Norris, Jr., and Donald C. Jackson. *Heavy Ground: William Mulholland and the St. Francis Dam Disaster.* Berkeley: University of California Press. 2015.

Jackson, Donald C., and Norris Hundley Jr. "Privilege and Responsibility: William Mulholland and the St. Francis Dam Disaster." *California History* 82, no. 3 (2004): 8–47.

Kahrl, William. *Water and Power: The Conflict over Los Angeles' Water Supply in the Owens Valley.* Berkeley: University of California Press, 1982.

Kleinsorge, Paul L. *The Boulder Canyon Project: Historical and Economic Aspects.* Stanford, CA: Stanford University Press, 1941.

Libecap, Gary D. *Owens Valley Revisited: A Reassessment of the West's First Great Water Transfer.* Stanford, CA: Stanford Economics and Finance, 2007.

Lillard, Richard G. *Eden in Jeopardy: Man's Prodigal Meddling with His Environment; the Southern California Experience.* New York: Alfred A. Knopf, 1966.

Mulholland, Catherine. *William Mulholland and the Rise of Los Angeles.* Berkeley: University of California Press, 2000.

Nadeau, Remi A. *The Water Seekers.* Garden City, NY: Doubleday, 1950.

Orsi, Jared. *Hazardous Metropolis: Flooding and Urban Ecology in Los Angeles.* Berkeley: University of California Press, 2004.

Ostrom, Vincent. *Water and Politics: A Study of Water Policies and Administration in the Development of Los Angeles.* Los Angeles: Haynes Foundation, 1953.

Outland, Charles F. *Man-Made Disaster: The Story of St. Francis Dam.* Glendale, CA: A. H. Clark, 1963.

Reisner, Marc. *Cadillac Desert: The American West and Its Disappearing Water.* New York: Viking, 1986.

Sauder, Robert A. *The Lost Frontier: Water Diversion in the Growth and Destruction of Owens Valley Agriculture.* Tucson: University of Arizona Press, 1994.

Stevens, Joseph E. *Hoover Dam: An American Adventure.* Norman: University of Oklahoma Press, 1988.

Turhollow, Anthony F. *A History of the Los Angeles District, U.S. Army Corps of Engineers, 1898–1965.* Los Angeles: U.S. Army Engineer District, 1975.

Walton, John. *Western Times and Water Wars: State, Culture, and Rebellion in California.* Berkeley: University of California Press, 1992.

Wilbur, Ray Lyman, and Northcutt Ely. *The Hoover Dam Documents.* 2nd ed. Washington: U.S. Government Printing Office, 1948.

Worster, Donald. *Rivers of Empire: Water, Aridity, and the Growth of the American West.* New York: Pantheon Books, 1985.

ACKNOWLEDGMENTS

The authors of this volume wish to thank the following colleagues and institutions for their assistance: John Cahoon, Betty Uyeda, Jenny Watts, Erin Chase, Brian Moeller, Blake Gumprecht, David Keller, Terri Garst, Jessica Kim; we thank the John Randolph Haynes and Dora Haynes Foundation and USC Dornsife College for subvention assistance, which allowed us to bring this book to Open Access with the University of California Press, and the Huntington-USC Institute on California and the West. We are also grateful to Niels Hooper and Bradley Depew of UC Press for guiding this project to fruition, and to our copyeditor, Bonita Hurd.

FIGURE 39. This rare photograph may depict the authors of this volume pursuing their research.
Courtesy of the Los Angeles Public Library Photo Collection.

INDEX